D1095265

The Political Principles of Robert A. Taft

The

Political

Principles

of

Robert A. Taft

by

Russell Kirk

&

James McClellan

A Project of The Robert A. Taft Institute of Government

FLEET PRESS CORPORATION
New York

Jacket photograph by © KARSH, *Ottawa*

Designed by Harvey Satenstein

MANUFACTURED IN THE UNITED STATES OF AMERICA

"BEFORE our system can claim success, it must not only create a people with a higher standard of living, but a people with a higher standard of character—character that must include religious faith, morality, educated intelligence, self-restraint, and an ingrained demand for justice and unselfishness. In our striving for material things, we must not change those basic principles of government and of personal conduct which create and protect the character of a people. . . . We cannot hope to achieve salvation by worshipping the god of the standard of living."

ROBERT A. TAFT

"A 1944 Program for the Republicans"

Introductory Note

◆━◆◆◆━◆

THIS BOOK WAS UNDERTAKEN AT THE REQUEST OF The Robert
A. Taft Institute of Government—of which, since its foundation in 1961, Mrs. Preston Davie has been chairman. At Yale,
in 1947, Senator Taft told the alumni, "The American people
seem to be doing less and less thinking for themselves and they
seem to have less and less knowledge of the history and basic
principles of the American Republic. . . . Public opinion is
formed without any real knowledge or analysis of the facts of
the issues."

As a non-partisan educational organization, the Taft Institute has endeavored in a number of ways to diminish the ignorance and apathy ·to which Senator Taft referred. The
Institute hopes to stimulate public understanding of the processes and problems of free government and of the American
constitutional structure.

A principal activity of the Institute has been the sponsorship
of seminars for elementary and secondary teachers. Of these
seminars on practical politics, the Cincinnati *Enquirer* has
remarked editorially, "There hardly could be a more fitting
memorial to the late Senator Robert A. Taft, who believed with

all his heart that a knowledgeable electorate is the surest route to good government, than the Robert A. Taft Institute of Government."

Also the Institute intends to publish materials related to its general aim of impartial political education. The present volume, describing Robert Taft's political convictions and influence, is the first accomplishment in this publication-program.

In addition to a research-grant from the Taft Institute, the authors thank Emory University for a generous contribution toward the costs of preparing the manuscript.

The authors are grateful for permission to examine the Robert A. Taft Papers in the Library of Congress. Several correspondents of Senator Taft have allowed the authors to quote from their letters.

For critical readings of this study, the authors are indebted to Mrs. Preston Davie, Representative Robert Taft, Jr., and Mr. Charles Brown—not, of course, that these readers necessarily concur in all the judgments of the authors.

Robert A. Taft was an upright champion of his party, but also he was something more—a champion of the principles of order, justice, and freedom. The trustees, advisors, and staff of the Taft Institute, and the authors of this volume, believe that Americans of all political persuasions will benefit from some attention to Taft's influence upon twentieth-century politics.

R.K. & J.McC

Contents

[ix]

CHAPTER I

The Political Principles of
Robert A. Taft

A Politician of Principle

Taft's Memory

BEING SERVILE TO NO ONE, Robert Alphonso Taft chose to be
called a politician, rather than a public servant. This is an
account of the principles of a party leader whose honesty and
intelligence transcended the controversies of the hour, and
whose influence upon American practical politics deserves
study.

No very thorough life of Taft has been published as yet, nor
any collection of his speeches. The authors of this handbook
hope that some day a careful and lengthy biography may
appear, and that Taft's more important addresses may be
disinterred from the *Congressional Record* and old newspaper
files. In the present book there will be found chiefly an analysis
of Taft's political beliefs.

It is neither as a picturesque figure nor as an orator that Taft
will endure; so Taft's ideas matter more than those personal
details relished by the biographer. In private life, Taft was a
good, shy, honorable man, innocent of eccentricities or of any
tragic flaw; although he spoke lucidly and carefully, he possessed no high eloquence. The significance of his life must be

1

found in the courage and the sound political sense which he displayed during his fourteen years in the United States Senate.

This present volume is not the history of a political career, nor yet a series of posthumous "position papers." Avoiding, so far as possible, the Serbonian bog of party hostilities, the authors of this book endeavor to describe the lasting contribution which Taft made to responsible political party, to the cause of ordered freedom, to the maintenance of justice, to the problems of labor, to the American economy, and to the formation of foreign policy. With such an approach, it is not possible to remain always chronological; yet we hope that the reader will find a systematic exposition of Taft's convictions more useful than would be a laborious chronicle of his stand on many issues, great or small, during the administrations of three presidents.

Robert Taft was no political speculator, but a busy public man immersed in practical matters of state; he published no regular manual of his opinions. Even his private correspondence, now mostly in the Library of Congress, contains few references to political first principles. He did write, indeed, one slim volume, *A Foreign Policy for Americans*, at a time when it appeared possible that he might be nominated by the Republicans for the presidency; and he participated very successfully in a series of radio debates with Representative T. V. Smith, his talks and Professor Smith's being published together in a volume entitled *Foundations of Democracy*. For the rest, however, his thought must be extracted from the immense mass of his remarks in the *Congressional Record* and his other political addresses, and from occasional articles he wrote for magazines. In that considerable task, the present authors were engaged for more than two years.

Like Edmund Burke, Robert Taft examined the foundations of society only with reluctance. A man of law, and not of metaphysics, he accepted American society as fundamentally sound; and his guiding principle was the rule of law. The federal Constitution, the legal institutions of America, and the traditions of the civil social order were the living rock upon which his convictions were founded. It was his labor to defend, and prudently to improve piecemeal, the American political and economic structure into which he had been born, and in the goodness of which he thoroughly believed. He stood as a practitioner of what has been called the "Great Tradition" of politics, maintaining justice through a healthy tension of order and freedom; so far as one may refer to a philosophical or a religious sanction for his beliefs, it was that complex of Christian and classical concepts of a moral order, right and duty, charity and justice. (Taft himself, it may be remarked, did not think of his own convictions as a "system.") As Tocqueville observed, the United States of America is governed for the most part by a kind of institutional aristocracy of lawyers, schooled in precedent and due process. Robert Taft was an eminent member of that body of republican governors.

In political opposition until the last six months of his life, Taft never took any executive office, and so is more important as a critic than as an architect of national policy. Several important legislative measures, nevertheless, were his work— most notably the Taft-Hartley Act governing labor-management relationships, and his part in the enactment of the first post-war federal public-housing measure. In terms of industry and practical intelligence, he was perhaps the ablest senator of this century; in influence over his party (for all that he never received its presidential nomination) and over public opinion generally, he was a man of power. Had he not been a man of high principle, his power might have been greater still. As an exemplar of American political rectitude and ability, he deserves to be remembered.

Yet for the crowd, Taft had no charisma. There was in him nothing of Theodore Roosevelt's magnetism, or of Franklin Roosevelt's beguiling public charm. His own father's wit and humor were not Robert Taft's—not in public. Most of the time, Taft seemed to the crowd a stiff and sober figure— benign, perhaps, but not constituted to warm one's heart. He could win Ohio elections thumpingly; still, like the Venetian

Glass Nephew, he did not know how to play. The dema-
gogue's arts were not his, nor the heroic attitudes of the
Periclean master of men. "Taft has been called a poor politician," a friendly observer wrote. "In a conventional sense, he
is. He not only lacks glamor, he scorns it—'there is so little
underneath it.' "[1]

And—what is not always the highroad to political success—
he regularly spoke his mind. When told that he was tactless, he
replied with characteristic simplicity, "It is not honest to be
tactful."[2] As much as Calhoun, and more than Webster or
Clay, he declined to sacrifice his principles to prospects of
glory; and like those Silver Age senators, he was fixed by his
steadfastness never to rise to executive authority. Like the
Adams Presidents, Taft was in the habit of uttering unpalat-
able truths. Robert Taft—who had in him little of the poet—
never may have read Yeats's poem "The Leaders of the
Crowd," but he disdained the cajoling of Demos as much as
did Yeats:

> They must to keep their certainty accuse
> All that are different of a base intent;
> Pull down established honour; hawk for news
> Whatever their loose fantasy invent
> And murmur it with bated breath, as though
> The abounding gutter had been Helicon
> Or calumny a song.

The man's independence of thought and action, too, though
it secured his election three times to the Senate and gave him
intellectual ascendancy within his party, did not open to him
the doors of the White House. He came very near to being
made President; in his last contest for the Republican nomination, he would have succeeded but for the abrupt introduction
into Republican politics of a triumphant military man.

Even within his party, Taft's blunt and able honesty was as
much handicap as advantage, in the competition for executive
power. Robert Taft was not supple—nor, when his first principles were concerned, given to compromise. Some of his

Republican competitors sincerely disagreed with him on matters of importance; but others who opposed his nomination were uneasy with his very uprightness and ability. For Senator Robert Taft could not be counted upon to accept and to grant favors, or to perform especial services for those possessing the means to advance him. It was patent that in the presidency he would be governed only by his own mind and conscience; no man, however much influence and money he might have, would be able to look to Taft for peculiar consideration of his particular interests. And as the middle of the twentieth century approached, swelling Washington might remind one of the prophecy of Henry Adams, in his novel *Democracy*. Rascally old Baron Jacobi, in that picture of the capital after the Civil War, predicts with relish, " 'I do much regret that I have not yet one hundred years to live. If I could then come back to this city, I should find myself very content—much more than now. I am always content where there is much corruption, and *ma parole d'honneur!*' broke out the old man with fire and gesture, 'the United States will then be more corrupt than Rome under Caligula; more corrupt than the Church under Leo X; more corrupt than France under the Regent!' "

If imperial Washington, during Taft's fourteen years there, had not arrived quite at the condition foretold by Jacobi, still the political apparatus could be employed to enrich or to ruin whole vast interests. For some people, the trouble with Taft as presidential possibility was not merely that Taft stood personally incorruptible: that defect was shared by certain other men with an eye upon the White House. No, Taft's trouble was that Taft always would make his own decisions, without much need of privy advice; and that Taft *knew*—understood the whole workings of the federal machinery, and how interests would be affected by legislation and executive policy. Such a person in executive authority must be awkward to manipulate.

There existed other reasons, too—some of them accidental— why Robert Taft never obtained his party's presidential nomination. No man ever was better prepared for assuming the presidency; and yet Taft's nearest approach to executive power came in his last months, when, though he had lost the Republican nomination and the presidential chair to General Eisenhower, it was Taft's experienced hand that formed national policy for some months in 1953. One thinks again of that tragi-comedy *Democracy*, and smiles wryly. Of course President Eisenhower was a man far more amiable than Adams's fictitious President called the Hoosier Stonecutter; and Senator Robert A. Taft was at the antipodes, morally, from the fictitious Senator Silas P. Ratcliffe. Yet as in the novel, a President who was a political tyro and innocent came under the indispensable influence of a veteran senator who had been his archrival; and presently the Senator was shaping every important domestic policy. At the end, Robert Taft had become, as Walter Lippmann put it, a "prime minister."

In political structures like that of Britain, where a party's parliamentary leader becomes prime minister if that party takes office, it would have gone otherwise, and Taft would have been President. But few eminent members of Congress have proceeded directly to the White House. Taft had as good a claim to the chief honor which American party can bestow as any American politician ever possessed. Yet that claim did not suffice. As candidate, Taft would have run a stronger race than did Landon or Willkie or Dewey—or so it appears in retrospect; indeed, it seems virtually certain that he would have defeated Truman in 1948, had he been chosen candidate. Where Dwight Eisenhower succeeded, Taft too might have won—if by a smaller margin. However that may be, one can only guess what sort of President Robert Taft might have been. But this politician of principle remains sufficiently important without that distinction.

"In my poor, lean, lank face nobody has ever seen any cabbages sprouting out. These are disadvantages all, taken together, that the Republicans labor under. We have to fight this battle upon principle and upon principle alone."[3] So Abraham Lincoln, whom Taft much admired, had said generations earlier. Taft and his party labored under disadvantages quite as heavy as Lincoln's, from 1932 to 1952. All those years, Taft fought his battle upon principle; and, against odds, now and again he triumphed. In 1939, Taft set out to rebuild his enfeebled party upon a foundation of principle, as an instrument of resistance to the New Deal.

This book deals with those years, although we are concerned more with the views Taft expressed than with party struggles. This is no biography; but it is necessary, in summary fashion, to set down here some account of Taft's political formative years in Ohio, before he stood tall in Washington— and of the circumstances of his entry into the Senate. For Taft did not enter national politics until he was nearly fifty years old.

Ohio Politics

The bald facts about this political leader are set down easily enough. Born at Cincinnati in 1889, the son of a President of the United States, he came of a family long conscientiously interested in public affairs and known for integrity, simplicity of life, and conservative opinions. Although small beside the fortunes of such recent political families as the Rockefellers and the Kennedys, Taft's private means always were sufficient to maintain him in political independence and to allow him to devote as much time as he liked to political activity.

He took his bachelor's degree from Yale in 1910,* and his law degree from Harvard in 1913. During the First World War (being rejected for military service) and shortly thereafter, he was active in the United States Food Administration and the American Relief Administration. He entered the lower house of the Ohio General Assembly in 1921, became Republican floor leader of that body in 1925, and was elected speaker

---

* Although one might not guess it from his speeches, Taft had been a remarkably good student of the classics and of humane letters, in his college years, under distinguished professors.

in 1926. He served in the Ohio Senate during 1931 and 1932. Although defeated in the Roosevelt landslide at the end of 1932, he remained eminent in Ohio's Republican party, so that in 1936 he was his state's favorite-son candidate for the Republican presidential nomination.

Politically, his was the "high old Roman virtue"; like certain Roman republican leaders, he was virtually a conscript father. The large following of William Howard Taft had expected the able son (to whom the Chief Justice often confided his private political reflections) to assume his father's place in the Republican party. William Howard Taft—successively Ohio judge, federal solicitor-general, federal circuit judge, professor of law, president of the Philippine Commission, civil governor of the Philippines, Secretary of War, professor again, President of the United States, and Chief Justice of the Supreme Court—found his modest and busy son, for all that, by no means eager to seek national political preferment.

"Bob does not write so often," the Chief Justice had mentioned in 1925, "for he seems to be very busy. I have no doubt he will conclude to refuse to run [for Congress] again."[4] Refuse he did—and took no part in national affairs while his father lived. "The vacancy created by [Senator] Burton's death leaves the question of his successor," Chief Justice Taft had written in 1929, the year he died, "and I don't think that Bob thinks the time is auspicious or that he would care to be in the Senate just now. His professional work is such that it would be very hard for him to give so much time as would be required for him to live in Washington."[5]

In state politics, however, Robert Taft took a considerable hand from 1920 to 1938. He had commenced as a Republican precinct worker; his terms in the Ohio House had established his reputation for political ability. In the Ohio Senate, he became known as expert in fiscal matters, attracting much attention throughout the state by his determined endeavor to revise Ohio's antiquated tax system.

While in the General Assembly, he rewrote the law of

taxation for city, county, and school finances. The chief aim of his bill, he explained, was "to relieve cities from restrictions which have made most of them bankrupt."[6] Obtaining sufficient support to override the governor's veto, Taft became known for his talents in legislative leadership; it is less widely recognized that in matters of finance he was an advocate of equitable reform.

In 1930, he served as chairman of the special joint tax commission of the legislature, which sponsored a program to repeal the old personal-property tax in Ohio and to enact a new classified tax on personal property, tangible and intangible. This task completed, Taft retired temporarily from politics after his defeat for re-election in the Democratic landslide of 1932.

Returning to his law practice, he declined for six years to run for office. Yet he came forward as an eminent private citizen when an effort was made to undo his tax reforms. The triumphant Democrats in the legislature had proposed a popular referendum to the effect that the Ohio constitution might be amended to decrease the rate of taxation levied upon real estate and tangible personal property. Schools, counties, and cities being dependent on the general property tax, Taft saw that this proposed reduction would nullify his earlier improvement of the tax structure. "Now I am an advocate of economy in governmental expenditures," he stated in a speech on October 11, 1933, "but unless we are prepared to scrap our schools and cities, and go back fifty years to primitive conditions, I would say that the cut proposed is absolutely impossible. . . . There are many people who seem to feel that economy in government can be carried to any length. But like everything else, it is really a question of degree, and I do not believe the people want the absolute essentials of government eliminated."[7]

Although he opposed this lowering of taxes, still Taft was attacked by his opponents as a spokesman for the rich and well-born. "He did a remarkably skillful job," wrote a contributor to the *New Republic*, years later, "of cleaning up the finances of the State. But one couldn't help noticing that in the course of restoring 'stability,' he advocated shifting the main tax burden to the poor."[8]

Like most of what was published about Taft in liberal journals of opinion, this was an unjust judgment upon Taft's motives. As he saw the proposed referendum on the property tax, it was in reality a device to clear the way for the enactment of a state sales tax, to which he was firmly opposed—and which, whatever its merits, lies more heavily upon the poor than upon the affluent. "In fact, this amendment seems to me a fraud on the people of the state," he said. "It purports to be a reduction in taxes, but it really means that after a period of bankruptcy for our schools, cities, and counties, and the permanent impairment of the credit of Ohio, there will be other taxes probably less equally divided and more burdensome than those that are being abolished."[9]

Such directness gave the man strong influence; and in Ohio, during those years, he made his reputation for probity and talent; clearly, he was a man fit to judge and to lead. "In back of the broad revision of Ohio's tax system, started on its perilous course through the House and Senate today," wrote the editors of the Cleveland *Plain Dealer*, in 1931, "stands the personality of its chief sponsor, Senator Robert A. Taft of Cincinnati. This tax code, unless changed beyond all semblance of its original form, will go down tagged as the Taft revision. His work, leadership, and inspiration have so dominated the committee that formed the bill that the whole legislature instinctively looks to him for guidance. . . . It is not depreciating any other member to say that Taft has the finest mind in the Ohio General Assembly. He is an indefatigable worker. He has inherited the traditional greatness of the Taft intellect. . . . He is the type of man all too rare in public life. Ohio is likely to make use of his fine mind in higher office before long—an office like the governorship or a seat in the United States Senate."[10]

The Face of the New Deal

Had the New Deal seemed less revolutionary in character, probably Robert Taft would have remained a Cincinnati lawyer. As Richard Rovere wrote (however mordantly) much later, Taft "is industrious, prudent, monogamous, proper in speech and comportment, law-abiding, church-going and presumably God-fearing, a good provider, a believer in education, a tree-grower, a good caretaker of the temple of the soul."[11] Taft exhibited no burning political ambition, and he disliked controversy, publicity, and what H. L. Mencken called "the art of boob-bumping." Except for the redoubtable name of Taft, few would have expected this quiet man of law to assume command of a national party.

Yet Taft stood for the Senate, and within the Senate became the real Republican leader, principally because no one else was effectively resisting those innovations of Roosevelt which Taft believed to be ruinous to the American republic. Even so, six years of the New Deal had elapsed before Taft stepped forward.

A generation after the triumph of Franklin Roosevelt, not everyone can remember the political passion of those years, nor the early thoroughgoing radicalism of many of Roosevelt's close advisers. The Great Depression had released the winds of fanatic ideology. Germany, Italy, Japan, and lesser powers—indeed, most modern states—had succumbed to one or another form of dictatorship; Soviet Russia, under the dread mastery of Stalin, scowled ferociously on the verge of Europe; France was near to anarchy; even Britain was shaken by strange doctrines. Roosevelt, though no radical by instinct or on principle, feared during his first administration that such as Huey Long might rise to authority in this hour, and so he stole the demagogues' clothes—and their thunder—by sweeping political and economic innovations. Around Roosevelt, such gentlemen as Hopkins, Tugwell, Wallace, and a score more were enthusiasts for fundamental alteration of American society, to be achieved almost instanter through positive law; moderates like Raymond Moley departed aghast from the administration.

"Most American radicals who were actively interested in extreme measures had long held the support of Socialists or of Communists," Professor Edgar Eugene Robinson writes of this period. "Mr. Roosevelt was neither. But in his emotional appeals, he was depending on the support of widespread discontent to further his own particular program of revolutionary control. . . . On the other hand, the radicals were not convinced of the soundness of Franklin Roosevelt's program, even though they praised it. They knew it for what it was—the result of the planning of a combination of discordant elements that were bound to the party machinery of the North as well as to the ultra-conservatives of the South. . . . Furthermore, throughout his years in office men of Communist sympathy had access to the President—and he listened to them."[12]

Such counsel, and such domestic policies, Robert Taft dreaded; and he discerned, too, the beginning of the drift toward deep involvement in European affairs that was to end in war. Herbert Hoover, from his enforced retirement, had been Roosevelt's only formidable opponent ever since 1932— as Roosevelt himself said privately. Thus as Robert Taft commenced to take a part in national affairs, his talents made him a leader of the opposition without any very conscious seeking for authority on his own behalf.

Representative Robert Taft, Jr., remarks to the present writers that his father thought it altogether possible that a second major depression might follow upon the partial recovery of the early Roosevelt years. In such circumstances, almost certainly the demand for collectivistic measures would increase; and bulwarks must be erected against such an eventuality and such an ideology. His stern criticism of the New Deal was intended, therefore, not simply to restrain Roosevelt and his followers, but also to forestall a second assault upon the American pattern of freedom and order. For similar reasons, he declined to approve the doctrine of pure *laissez-faire:* some Rooseveltian measures had been necessary reforms, and to undo them would be to invite more radical remedies during any new economic crisis.

So, early in 1935, Taft commenced that systematic criticism of the New Deal which eventually was to make him the national leader of the opposition. His most important speech during this period was made to the Chamber of Commerce of Warren, Ohio, in April. There Taft compared the New Deal to "one of those fabulous creatures of Herodotus, with the head of a dragon and the body of a cow." The New Deal smacked of socialism, which "is absolutely contrary to the whole American theory on which this country was founded, and which has actually made it the most prosperous country in the world. It is inconsistent with democratic government. . . . Communism, Fascism, and Hitlerism have destroyed a system like ours in many European countries, and substituted a form of despotic socialism. . . . As far as we can judge, socialism will not work. There is no man and no group of men intelligent enough to coordinate and control the infinitely numerous and complex problems involved in the production, consumption, and daily lives of one hundred and twenty million individualistic and educated people." He attacked the fallacies of Huey Long and Father Coughlin—which fallacies he found in the New Deal also.

"Some of the wealthy have been too wealthy," he continued, "but the despoiling of their wealth would hardly solve the problem. In 1929 the total income of the United States was approximately eighty-five billion dollars. All of the dividends on all of the stocks, all of the interest on all of the bonds, and all of the rents on all of the real estate only totalled approximately fifteen and one-half billion dollars. If we took all the wealth, and divided the income in that prosperous year throughout the entire population, it would not have added more than twenty per cent to the average man's income, and it would finally destroy the entire incentive to build up the savings and investments which produced this wealth."

Taft proceeded to strong assaults upon the Tennessee Valley Authority, the National Recovery Act, and the Roosevelt agricultural program: these were meant to destroy competition. Of the NRA, he declared, "the only defensible features of this program seem to me the abolition of child labor and the establishment of minimum wage scales, which might be done independently of NRA." Moreover, these programs were ineffectual. "Like most revolutionary measures, the NRA and AAA have served the additional bad purpose of retarding recovery. They have unquestionably raised prices, and I believe that, except in abnormal situations, this artificial raising of prices has destroyed more purchasing power than it has created, and has prevented the natural increase in business resulting from cheaper products."

Beyond these measures, nevertheless, Taft was not in thorough disagreement with the New Deal in 1935. Those New Deal policies calculated to restore the American business system, Taft readily accepted. "Some of its measures," he conceded, "attempt to remove the faults seen in that system and offer true reform. . . . I think no one can question the wisdom of the government loaning money to businesses and individuals to tide them over a depression, when the private machinery of lending broke down. The RFC, the Home Owners' Loan Corporation, and the farm loan boards have . . . prevented sales and liquidation which would . . . have caused greatly increased social problems." Taft also believed that "the government should undoubtedly carry on public works on an increased scale in times of depression. The only difficulty with the public works program is that its importance has been exaggerated, because the amount required to prime the pump is far greater than any government can afford or carry through without danger of governmental bankruptcy."

Nor was Taft inflexibly opposed to governmental interference in all circumstances. "Social conditions under some circumstances," he said, "demand government interference. We have not hesitated in the past to regulate or prohibit monopoly, to encourage trade unions, to encourage cooperative dealing by farmers and laborers, to tax wealth and income on a progressively higher rate, to regulate banking and currency. . . . I believe, therefore, that the Stock Exchange Control Act was a wise measure, and I see no objection to the control of the principles of banking credit by the government instead of by the Federal Reserve Banks. Banking has always been the subject of government control under all systems, and the exact measure of that control is one of degree."

The American system is not without abuses, he declared. When the employer had too arbitrary a hand, low wages and the employment of children had resulted. "The abolition of child labor by constitutional amendment should be carried through, and minimum wage laws should be encouraged nationally and throughout the states."

He would allow, besides, experiment in the fields of social security and unemployment insurance—so long as such programs should not be allowed to destroy personal incentives, or grow so costly as to drive up prices, draw on reserves, and compel borrowing against the future. "The real question regarding old age pensions and unemployment insurance is whether we can carry the burden without reducing the standard of living of everyone else in the country. . . . I believe the present bill perhaps goes too far, and we should begin with somewhat smaller payments, and see how they work."

Only through the recovery of business could the Depression be terminated. "If natural recuperative forces are really at work, we may have prosperity in spite of the New Deal. Its real danger may, therefore, be far more in the political field than in the economic."

Concluding, Taft demanded that experiment in governmental operation of business be abandoned, "unless it is absolutely required by intolerable social conditions in a particular industry. Let us abandon the idea that any good result can come of a redistribution of the wealth. These ideas, advanced strenuously outside of the administration, and encouraged by many of the New Deal policies, will lead not to recovery, not to reform, but to revolution."[13]

What Taft said in this Warren speech had been said before, for the most part, by Herbert Hoover, Glenn Frank, and other opponents of the New Deal, Republican and Democratic. But Robert Taft was a rising man, whom no one could blame for the Depression; and he spoke convincingly. Ohio now expected him to go far.

From Cincinnati to Washington

By 1936, the Great Depression approached its seventh year; the full economic recovery promised by President Roosevelt had not come to pass; and the revolution dreaded by Taft still was conceivable. This was the year, nevertheless, when Franklin Roosevelt's power was at its zenith. In speech after speech, throughout Ohio, Taft declared that President Roosevelt's programs were prolonging the Depression out of political expediency—and injuring the fabric of American society.

In an address to the Young Republicans of Lawrence County, on April 4, 1936, Taft forcefully repeated his belief that the New Deal's fundamental postulates must be opposed. "I have frequently said that the Republican platform and the Republican candidates must be uncompromisingly opposed to the New Deal. . . . There are many measures designed to meet the emergency, and cure abuses in the old system, which the Republican Party should carry on and develop. But there is an underlying philosophy in the principal measures of the New Deal which desires to effect a complete revolution in the whole American business and constitutional system under which this country has prospered for 150 years. Against that philosophy and the measures which attempt to carry it out, the Republican candidates must be wholeheartedly and violently opposed. That policy is one of planned economy."

The concept of a planned economy, he continued, constituted the basis of socialism, and was inimical to American practices and traditions. "The basis of the American business and constitutional system is political and economic liberty, with equal opportunity to improve one's condition by one's own effort. It is a system based on individual initiative, individual freedom to conduct agriculture, commerce, manufacture, in fact on rugged individualism. It attempts to reward by increase in material welfare those qualities of intelligence, ability, industry, and genius, which played such a great part in building up the nation as we see it today. Government is conceived as a keeper of the peace, a referee of controversies, and an adjustor of abuses; not as a regulator of the people, or their business and personal activities."[14]

In the same year, Taft developed a second political theme: that the New Deal was a practical failure. In a speech at Ardmore, Pennsylvania, on October 21, 1936, he stated: "Apparently his [President Roosevelt's] single appeal is that the country is more prosperous today than it was in 1932, and therefore the Democratic policies have improved the conditions of the people. He ignores the existence of nine million unemployed, and the fact that no country can really be prosperous while such unemployment exists. He also has difficulty pointing to the measures which have produced prosperity. It cannot have been the NRA and AAA and related matters, for these were nullified by the Supreme Court, and improvement began from the day they were nullified. It cannot have been any economic policy supposed to increase exports, because exports are less than they were in 1932. The President's claims seem to boil down to the single proposition that prosperity has been produced by the liberal expenditure of government money."[15]

In the midst of such assaults upon the New Deal, Robert Taft had become Ohio's "favorite son" candidate for the Republican presidential nomination. In the May, 1936, primary, forty-seven of Ohio's fifty-two delegates elected expressed their support of Taft; the rest endorsed Senator Borah of Idaho. At the Republican National Convention, Taft was not a serious contender for the nomination, however; the Ohio delegation and Taft's scattered admirers in other states made no strong endeavor to wrest the nomination from Alfred Landon. But a party which could settle upon no stronger candidate than Governor Landon was in the sear and yellow leaf.

By the elections of 1936, the Republicans were reduced to an impotent minority, deprived of true leadership and direction. Alfred M. Landon carried only two states. So enormous was the Democratic victory that half of the states elected no Republican congressmen at all; and so enfeebled were the Republicans in the House of Representatives that sometimes they were unable to muster one-fifth of the membership, to force a rollcall vote. So overwhelming was the Democratic majority that thirteen Democratic representatives had to sit on the other side of the aisle, with Republicans. It appeared that the nation might come down to government by a single party—just what already had occurred in many European states.

Buoyed up by a fresh popular mandate, Roosevelt embarked in 1937 upon a bold new series of programs, beginning with the "court-packing scheme." It seemed to many—including conservative Democrats—that the whole American constitutional edifice might be brought down. Yet the opposition remained ineffectual, for the most part, despite Congress's rejection of Roosevelt's design upon the Supreme Court.

No one else had come forward to lead the Congressional opposition manfully; perhaps Robert Taft must. His speeches early in 1938 were those of a man who meant to enter the Senate. "We see in America today an attack on nearly every American principle," he emphasized in a speech at St. Clairsville, Ohio, on January 24, 1938. "These attacks are not particularly political attacks; we find them in pulpit, in magazines, in newspapers, and on the radio." In another speech he said, "In the guise of legislation to improve the condition of the people, we see an attack, probably not itself conscious of its direction, upon the political principles of American democracy. . . . In the mistaken belief that government can remove all poverty, redistribute all wealth, and bestow happiness on every citizen, measures are proposed which must destroy American democracy. . . ."[16]

Again, Taft did not denounce every feature of the New Deal; he distinguished between those "recovery" measures consonant with American political and economic principles, and those revolutionary innovations of the New Deal which threatened to tear the fabric of society or to retard economic recovery. He asserted that Republicans "believe completely in the humanitarian measures of the *original* New Deal, and propose to carry them forward with a better direct result to the workingman than has now been achieved."[17] Where economic planning was concerned, Taft opposed both the aims and the methods of the New Deal, but on matters of welfare and public relief he was in agreement, substantially, with New Deal palliatives. His point was this: the states, and not the federal government, should retain primary responsibility for works of welfare and relief.

More fundamentally, Taft did not believe that economic *recovery* could be produced by mere measures of relief, whether federal or state in application. Campaigning across Ohio, Taft insisted repeatedly that "the Administration's program has not worked. Business has declined 25 per cent; unemployment is increasing. Stocks have dropped faster than in 1929. We are in the midst of a depression."[18] A few days later he said, "We are a practical people. We may be interested in theory or we may not be. . . . Planned economy has not produced any prosperity equal to that which existed before 1928. In spite of manipulation of the currency, in spite of devaluing the dollar, in spite of deficits amounting to $15 billion and the pouring out of public funds, in spite of unlimited power given to regulate the farm industry, the coal industry, the utility industry, and the issue of securities, in spite of countless additional powers as great as could be granted within the constitution, we are faced today with complete failure."[19]

Indeed, the Roosevelt recession had commenced. Yearly average unemployment had affected 13,182,000 persons in 1932; by 1938, it was 10,936,265, and rising rapidly. The *American Federationist*, a publication of the American Federation of Labor, estimated in its April, 1939, issue that the unemployment figure for 1939 would be 11,470,262. The Department of Commerce reported in its *Survey of Current Business* that the monthly average of business failures was rising: 751 per month in 1937; 1,149 for February, 1938. The *Survey* also noted that in 1932 the monthly average of securities issued was valued at $27,133,000; it had been a monthly average of $666,839,000 in 1929. In 1933 the issuance of securities had dropped sharply, but thereafter had risen steadily through 1933, 1934, 1935, and 1936, to a peak of $99,477,-000 monthly average in 1937. Then commenced the recession: in 1938, the monthly average of securities issued fell abruptly to $40,852,000; by 1939, it would be only $23,571,000—worse than the year 1932, when Roosevelt had been elected President.

Despite this recession, the period was one of jubilation for Franklin Roosevelt. In his annual message to Congress, on January 4, 1939, Roosevelt was to boast that the United States "had now passed the period of internal conflict in the launching of our program of social reform. Our full energies may now be released to invigorate the processes of recovery in order to preserve our reforms."[20]

Taft held otherwise. The New Deal, he demonstrated statistically, had failed to restore full prosperity, and had succeeded only in undermining American institutions. He now adopted the practice of explaining his principles, and challenging those of the New Deal, through public debate. At such impromptu exchange, he was better than at formal speech-making; this brought him face to face repeatedly with champions of the New Deal, until as the years passed there were few who cared to encounter him after this fashion. His command of information was masterly, and his mind was quick at rejoinder.

The Ohio Republicans did what they would have liked to do earlier: they nominated Robert Taft to the United States

Senate in 1938. He stood against the incumbent Senator Robert J. Bulkley, a strong supporter of the New Deal, who readily accepted Taft's invitation to debate the issues before the public. That decision was Senator Bulkley's undoing.

In their second debate, for instance, Bulkley spent the larger part of his time deriding Taft, while his opponent, fortified with figures, delivered a searching analysis of New Deal failures. "At Marietta," Taft said, "I advanced the proposition that the New Deal had completely failed to solve the problems of the country; that it had promised prosperity in social security and that, as a matter of fact, it had brought about a condition which is even worse in many respects than it was five years ago. I cited the fact that unemployment had increased again, until today, according to AFL figures, the last I could get, it is eleven million, three or four hundred thousand. There are more people on the WPA today than there ever have been in the history of the state. The business indexes show about the same condition that existed five years ago after the first upturn from the previous depression. There is no indication that after all of this spending, there is any improvement whatever in the economic condition."

Senator Bulkley might have done well had he ignored these Taft arguments; imprudently, however, he chose to try to reply directly, with disastrous results. "Now we come back to the old absurdity," protested Bulkley, "that things are not better now than they were in 1933, and the old emphasis that there are eleven and a half million unemployed. There were fourteen million at least unemployed in 1932 and 1933 and probably more than that, for all we know. Now is it not better to have only eleven and a half million unemployed? I have quoted plenty of statistics and you know in your hearts that things are better now than they were in 1933."[21]

But the Ohio public was very much aware of the Roosevelt Recession, and was not heartened by the confession that *only* 11,500,000 Americans were unemployed. Robert Taft was elected to the Senate that autumn by a majority of 170,000 votes.

The statistical argument, nevertheless, had been only one of Taft's issues in the campaign. As he remarked in a post-election radio broadcast, his campaign had been essentially a protest against the *theories* of the New Deal. "There has been some suggestion," he said then, "that the result of the November election in Ohio was determined by local issues. As a matter of fact, both Governor Bricker and myself based our whole campaign on an anti-New Deal platform. We did not criticize merely New Deal methods. We openly asked the people to repudiate the basic principles which the New Deal adopted during the last two years, the principles of planned economy and government regulation of commerce, agriculture, and industry, and the arbitrary power demanded to carry out such a program. In 1937 the New Dealers pushed into the background the earlier humanitarian measures like old-age pensions, federal assistance to relief, unemployment insurance, and the like, and started a new course completely destructive of the American constitutional and social system as we have known it."[22]

Now Robert Taft—a fighting man when roused, for all his shyness—would carry the campaign into Washington.

———◆◆◆———

Notes, CHAPTER I

1. Benjamin Stolberg, "Robert A. Taft: American Liberal," *The American Mercury*, Vol. LXXI, No. 322 (October 1950), p. 391.

2. Quoted in Caroline Thomas Harnsberger, *A Man of Courage* (Chicago, 1952), p. 142.

3. See *The Collected Works of Abraham Lincoln* (edited by Roy P. Basler), Vol. II (New Brunswick, N.J., 1953), p. 506.

4. William Howard Taft to Helen Taft Manning, March 1, 1925. Helen Taft Manning Papers, Library of Congress.

5. William Howard Taft to Helen Taft Manning, November 3, 1929. Helen Taft Manning Papers, Library of Congress.

6. Robert A. Taft to Horace Taft, May 2, 1923. Robert A. Taft Papers, Library of Congress.

7. Speech before the Building and Loan Association, in convention, Deshler Hotel, Columbus, Ohio, October 11, 1933. Copy in Robert A. Taft Papers, Library of Congress.

8. Carroll Kilpatrick, "Taft: 20 Degrees Cooler Inside," *The New Republic*, Vol. 115, No. 25 (December 23, 1946), pp. 870–871.

9. Speech before the Building and Loan Association, *op. cit.*

10. Cleveland *Plain Dealer*, May 28, 1931.

11. Richard Rovere, "Taft: Is this the Best We've Got?," *Harper's Magazine*, Vol. 196, No. 1175 (April 1948), p. 290.

12. Edgar Eugene Robinson, *The Roosevelt Leadership, 1933–1945* (Philadelphia, 1955), pp. 181, 191, 227.

13. Robert A. Taft, "The New Deal: Recovery, Reform, and Revolution," speech delivered before the Warren, Ohio, Chamber of Commerce, April, 1935. Copy in Robert A. Taft Papers, Library of Congress.

14. Robert A. Taft, Speech before the Young Republican Club of Lawrence County, Ohio, April 4, 1936. Copy in Robert A. Taft Papers, Library of Congress.

15. Robert A. Taft, Speech at Ardmore, Pennsylvania, October 21, 1936. Copy in Robert A. Taft Papers, Library of Congress.

16. Speech at St. Clairsville, Ohio, as reported in the Cincinnati *Times-Star*, January 24, 1938; and speech at Cadiz, Ohio, as reported in the Cincinnati *Times-Star*, January 25, 1938.

17. Speech at Cleveland, Ohio, as reported in the Cincinnati *Enquirer*, January 30, 1938.

18. Speech at Youngstown, Ohio, as reported in the Cincinnati *Times-Star*, January 26, 1938.

19. As reported in the Cincinnati *Times-Star*, February 1, 1938.

20. *Public Papers of Franklin D. Roosevelt*, edited by Samuel Rosenman, Vol. 8 (New York, 1941), p. 7.

21. Debate of Taft and Bulkley at the Dayton Coliseum, Dayton, Ohio, October 14, 1938. Copy in Robert A. Taft Papers, Library of Congress.

22. Radio statement of Robert A. Taft, January 3, 1939. Copy in Robert A. Taft Papers, Library of Congress.

CHAPTER II

Foundations of Democracy

First Months in the Senate

ALREADY AN ACCOMPLISHED POLITICAL STRATEGIST, and known for his keen mind, Robert Taft was elevated to a position of leadership among Senate Republicans almost as soon as he took his seat in the Senate of the United States, in January, 1939. In short order, he had mastered the parliamentary tactics of that body. He was assigned to important committees ordinarily reserved for senior senators, including appropriations, banking and currency, and education and labor; he commenced to contend with some very knotty problems.

President Roosevelt's adherents found Taft to be a formidable opponent from the first. At the outset, Senator Taft had considerable part in stirring up a Congressional revolt which restricted the extension of the New Deal into areas as yet uninvaded. His first speech was in opposition to an appropriation for the colossal Gilbertsville Dam of the Tennessee Valley Authority. His dislike of this grandiose project was characteristic: he saw in such activities of TVA the diminution of private rights and American ways of life by the swelling mass-state. TVA already was proceeding far beyond its functions authorized by Congress—navigation and flood control— to become King Kilowatt, eliminating private utility companies, embarking on vast sales of electric power (and power,

24

in the long run, not water-generated but coal-generated, at that), and operating as an autonomous monopoly almost beyond any control by Congress. Professor Donald Davidson describes the Gilbertsville project, later called Kentucky Dam:

> Kentucky Dam was to be a mighty affair. Paducah, twenty-three miles downriver, would repose nervously in its shadow. Behind its wall, which was 206 feet high and over a mile and a half long, the waters of the Tennessee would be backed up for 184 miles, all the way to Pickwick Landing Dam. Its vast lake would stand, almost like the lagoon of geological ages past, on a straight north-and-south line across the width of Kentucky and Tennessee. Its reservoir would permanently retire from use 134,000 acres of land (not to speak of at least 100,000 more acres to be occasionally invaded for flood control), would cause the removal of some 3,500 families, and would completely drown out such Kentucky river towns as Birmingham and Newburg, and would vitally affect the arrangements of such places in Tennessee as Stribling, Danville, Johnsonville, Trotter's Ferry, Cuba Landing.
>
> These were all, of course, just little river villages, crossroads, or shipping points, beloved enough to their inhabitants, but lacking in industrial installations and therefore inexpensive to buy up. . . . The Big Sandy River and Duck River would become fresh-water estuaries, and Duck River bottoms, long famous for their corn crops, and other good bottom land along the Tennessee, would be invaded by water; and you could not grow good corn, in that country, except in the bottoms.[1]

Taft's part in the Gilbertsville debate is amusing and instructive, and foreshadowed his coming power in the Senate. Generally, Taft founded his practical objections to the dam on the lack of proven need, on the tremendous expense, and on its dubious efficacy in producing electric power. Much confusion existed in the minds of the dam's advocates as to whether this was a flood-control project or a power project. When the Democrats argued that Gilbertsville was intended for flood control, Taft upset them by showing that according to the dam's plans, it could be regarded only as a power project. He then added that it made little sense to call Gilbertsville a flood-control undertaking, for it would flood more than a hundred thousand acres of good land, at the lowest estimate, and much more eventually. "This dam is going to backwater back 186 miles. It is going to destroy, for all useful purposes, about 400,000 acres of the best farm land in Kentucky permanently."*

As for navigation, the Gilbertsville dam was liable to create hazards, rather than to facilitate river traffic. The Democratic majority in the Senate wished to spend $106 million on the dam; Taft suspected that eventually it would cost much more—and that the cost would be concealed, in part, by TVA's mysterious accounting system. Taft found absurd the notion of one behemoth dam. Why not a series of low dams, rather, practical for flood control and navigation? The real necessity on the Tennessee was flood control, not power; yet the Gilbertsville dam was to flood out whole towns.

In the course of the debate, Taft shook eminent Democratic senators. His first victim was Kenneth McKellar, of Tennessee. In the exchange, it became evident that Taft, pouring out statistics, knew much more about the project than did the senator from Tennessee (later to become himself a severe critic of many of TVA's activities); McKellar was provoked into a rejoinder, angry but ineffectual. To McKellar's aid, and to the rescue of the Gilbertsille design, came the formidable Senator Alben Barkley, who soon seemed even more confused than McKellar had been. Taft buried Barkley under facts and figures, and Barkley clearly experienced difficulty in following his adversary's argument. Chagrined, the senator from Kentucky accused Taft of having read his speech from manuscript—though actually Taft had spoken extemporaneously. Taft's startling ability to keep readily available in his memory a mass of detailed information was manifested in the Senate for the first time.

* *Congressional Record*, 76th Congress, 1st Session, Vol. 84, Part 2 (February 20, 1939), p. 1599.

An impartial auditor of the debate might have been led to suspect that McKellar, Barkley, and other champions of the Gilbertsville dam knew little about the whole plan except that it would result in a great deal of federal money being spent in Tennessee and Kentucky. "If there ever was a toy which had no other use except to amuse those who are playing with it," Taft concluded with the dry wit he occasionally displayed on the Senate floor, "Gilbertsville dam is that toy."

Though Taft won the debate, the Roosevelt administration's congressional majority carried the day, and eventually Kentucky Dam was completed. Yet the criticisms of Taft and those influenced by him are one reason why TVA remains solitary as an attempt to alter a whole region and a whole economy according to the conceptions of central political power. Grandiose planning of this sort, Taft believed, was contrary to the American political system; it could be achieved only through propaganda and compulsion.

During his early senatorial months, Taft also opposed increases in farm subsidies, and fought against increasing the powers of the Securities and Exchange Commission—although he approved the Commission's function of protecting the investor against fraud.

Expert in fiscal matters, Taft was remarkably useful in the Banking Committee. Quick to extract significance from complex statistics, he analyzed the evidence of the administration's officials and endeavored to expose fallacies in New Deal programs. He was a leader, too, in opposition to the continuance of the President's power to devalue the dollar.

His first major senatorial victory occurred in these early months of his career, when almost unaided he defeated President Roosevelt's "spending-lending" bill. Roosevelt's three-billion-dollar program was not merely a spending program, under the guise of lending, but was also, as Taft pointed out, a scheme to escape from the statutory debt limit and from the fiscal control of Congress. Taft complained in committee hearings and on the Senate floor that the bill amounted to a plan for placing the government permanently and increasingly in the management of American finance and industry. He demonstrated that the program could not repay its costs; and he exposed major flaws, against which he drafted amendments accepted by the Senate. The bill was so thoroughly dissected by Taft in the Senate that the House of Representatives declined to consider its remnants. As one commentator put it, "A large part of Mr. Taft's questioning in committee, and his speeches on the Senate floor, were so flatly put that they never were reported in the newspapers. . . . He humiliated Mr. Morgenthau, drove Administration experts and Senators into a raging silence. It was the New Deal's first big-money bill to be totally defeated."[2]

Thus Taft accepted the responsibilities that were heaped upon him, and unassumingly took up the leadership of the opposition. Fellow Republicans came to look upon him as "the man who would lead the Congressional Republicans out of their inertia and defeatism, reshape their program, and make them an articulate opposition to the liberals and international-ists of the New Deal and the Fair Deal."[3] In this, his colleagues seldom were disappointed. For fourteen years this man of courage and talent stood on the floor of the Senate chamber to resist the encroachments of the New Deal and the Fair Deal upon old liberties and institutions. Turning any blunder of Roosevelt or Truman into a victory for his party, Taft was to alter the whole drift of American society. It is not that he totally undid New Deal and Fair Deal: rather, he, more than any other man, compelled impulsive reformers to come to terms with reality and with the American pattern of politics. In part abandoned, in part restricted, in part reconciled with the American constitutional and economic system, the New Deal ceased to be a quasi-revolutionary ideology.

Practical Alternatives

Yet the accomplishment of Robert Taft was by no means one wholly of negation and restraint. Repeatedly, while in the

Senate, he was to draft closely-reasoned Republican party programs, offering alternatives to the administration's plans. He had commenced this work, indeed, shortly before election to the Senate.

On September 14, 1938, Taft had addressed the Ohio Republican Convention; he had begun by declaring that "the New Deal has utterly failed to solve the problems of the nation. It has no program to present except a demand for more power and the expenditure of vast amounts of borrowed money." The Republican party must present to the people a program which would restore prosperity and "see that prosperity reaches those to whom an improvement in condition is most essential." How might prosperity be achieved? Taft answered that "fundamentally, prosperity can only be restored by the stimulation of private industry. The greatest problem we have to face is that of unemployment, and unemployment cannot be solved by relief. It must be cured by putting more men and women to work in private industry and building up private industry to take care of them."

As for specific measures, Taft had suggested that "The first essential is a sound government financial policy, and we propose that the government balance its budget by reducing its expenses. This can be done without reducing the payments for relief and social security, which, after all, only amount to about two and a half billion dollars in a total budget of nine billion dollars."

Secondly, Taft had recommended that "The Republican Party . . . encourage men to go into business, to establish new industries, to enlarge existing industries, through a reduction of taxation. . . . The whole tax system should be revised to encourage and reward ingenuity, industry, genius and daring as those qualities have always been rewarded in the past." Generally speaking, "The entire government policy of hostility to private industry should be abandoned."

The farm problem, for example, could best be dealt with through "a complete restoration of the market. Limitation of production never has been successful in permanently increasing farm prices." More, "The government should take an active interest in finding new uses for farm products. It should coordinate the different credit agencies so that a farmer entitled to credit can borrow money without vast reams of red tape. It should develop a consistent and persistent policy of retiring land from strictly agricultural uses—at least to the extent that new land is created through irrigation projects. The farmer is at some disadvantage through our protective policy because the price of some of the things he buys is raised by the tariff while he has to sell some of his products in the world market. This justifies a subsidy which should take the form of benefits for soil conservation and subsidy for the planting of crops which bring about soil improvement. In short, the farmer should be assisted and encouraged to develop his own farm . . . without arbitrary dictation and bureaucratic regulation."

On the question of welfare, Taft had suggested that "to insure that relief not be used for local political purposes, the federal grant should be conditioned on a proper non-partisan administration in the localities." He also believed that "The Republican Party should pledge itself to provide an adequate and complete system of old-age pensions. . . . The Social Security Act should be amended to provide more adequate assistance from the Federal Government in that the state old-age pension system may be made complete and effective as intended under the Ohio law. . . . Under the present system Ohio employees and employers have paid into the Federal Government approximately $57 million up to June 1, 1938, and the state has only received back about $25 million. The rest has been invested in government bonds and the cash used to pay New Deal deficits."

Directing his attention to labor questions, Taft had asserted that "The Republican labor policy is definite and clear. It is substantially that urged by the American Federation of Labor. The Government has undertaken to protect by law the workman's right of collective bargaining free from any pressure from the employer and should continue to do so. I believe, however, that the Wagner Act should be amended by defining unfair labor practices on the part of employees as well as employers and by giving employers and employees the right to request elections and complain to the Board. I believe that the Board's functions should be divided between a prosecuting section and a judicial section. More than anything else, however, the labor relations policy of the Federal government should be impartial. The present Board has not only been openly hostile to employers but has favored one union over other unions." He added, "I am opposed to the fixing of wages by law or by government agency. Strikes may be a bad thing, but the freedom to strike seems to me essential to the preservation of workmen's rights. The Republican party should support a reasonable minimum wage in cases where conditions are such that collective bargaining is ineffective, and the administration of the wage-hour law should be confined to such cases."

Finally, Taft had told the Ohio Convention that "The prosperity of each group can be more effectively restored through a general restoration of prosperity rather than any direct assistance to that group. It can be more effectively restored by individual freedom and free competition under the American Constitution and the American way of life than by the importation of ideas from Russia or from Germany."[4]

On the eve of his election to the Senate, then, Taft had displayed an ability, almost unique among Republicans, to criticize the theories of his opponents while at the same time offering alternatives founded upon much thought and research. If Taft seemed complex or inconsistent to some critics, it was because, often, they failed to understand that Taft was engaged in applying old principles to new conditions. That he occasionally appeared to change his mind was merely evidence that he had made some new discovery as to how a difficulty might be met without abandoning tested general principles.

But he was not given to enunciating *new* general principles. As a senator, Taft's appeal was to the laws and the Constitution—never to abstractions, if it might be helped. Taft spoke more convincingly when defending the principles of economics and of constitutional precedent than when expounding political theories. He was in no sense an original political thinker. Rather, he was a lawyer who defended from conviction the American political inheritance; he was representative of what Daniel Boorstin calls the "givenness" of American political thought.

On one occasion or another, Taft's strong intellect was praised by those who disagreed, in large part, with his practical politics. As Arthur M. Schlesinger, Jr., wrote in 1947, "His saving grace is a clear-cut logical intelligence and a basic respect for fact, which undercut his own impulses toward dogmatism. Even his enemies respect his intellectual honesty and his reasoning powers."[5]

Although he was called "Mr. Republican," his leadership was founded less upon hot partisanship than upon intellect, learning, and diligence. He had no political machine behind him. "There have not been more than a half dozen men in high elective office during the past thirty years," one liberal critic wrote, "who have had as sound a grasp of the processes of government as he has. He knows government better than any President since Woodrow Wilson, and since he has learned what he knows from long legislative experience as well as from other universities, he might reasonably be given the edge over Wilson."[6]

Among his senatorial colleagues, Republican or Democratic, these qualities were so generally recognized in Taft that in 1946, Congress (with a Democratic majority) polled itself and chose Taft as its ablest member. There seemed to be no limit to his patience and his grasp of detail. As the Alsops—not friendly toward Taft, usually—said of him, "His industry is so unrelenting, his mind so indefatigable, that he did what no senator in memory has ever attempted. He familiarized himself with every significant domestic bill that came before the Senate. If the Republicans wanted amendments he drafted them; and where no bill met his requirements he went to work and wrote one himself."[7]

As the laborious years passed, Taft would continue to dominate the Republicans in Congress, despite his defeats at party presidential nominating conventions. Long before he became formal Republican leader in the Senate, *de facto*, he dominated Republican policy—indeed, more than Republican policy. In 1949, for instance, he would belong to a minority in Congress, and would have been rejected as presidential candidate by the Republicans. Nevertheless, as a political writer confessed in reluctant admiration, "Despite the sensational Truman Democratic election victory, Taft is again the most influential single member of the Senate. It is not excessive to say that he is the leader of the Senate; for practical purposes he has far more power than the unfortunate Scott Lucas of Illinois, who holds the title of Democratic floor chieftain but commands only a theoretical majority."[8]

One mark of Taft's practical talent was a readiness, rapidly acquired, to shift from one committee to another in the Senate, as new difficulties arose and old problems were diminished. Not content to remain on one committee gathering the privileges of seniority, he sought new questions to which he might direct his energies. Often he had the pick of any committee, but purposely involved himself in difficult concerns, at the risk of unpopularity with the public—as when, in his last year, Taft abandoned financial matters to join the Foreign Relations Committee.

Throughout his Senate years, Taft would seek to lift his party above opportunism and to fix it to firm principles. He was a man of party because, like Burke, he understood that in modern society freedom and order cannot endure without the apparatus of responsible political party. In serving party, he meant to serve his country; there was no inconsistency in loyalty to both.

Debates with T. V. Smith

Only once, and that early in his senatorial office, did Taft find time to undertake a systematic written exposition of his principles. In his first term, he agreed to debate in a series of radio broadcasts with Professor T. V. Smith, then Congressman-at-large from Illinois. These debates were promptly published under the title *Foundations of Democracy*, a book long out of print.

Dr. Smith, a distinguished professor of philosophy, possessed considerable charm, wit, and learning; and he knew how to win an audience. He had an immense fund of apt quotation—an art at which Taft frequently was inept or inaccurate. Supporter of the New Deal though he was, Smith was not a doctrinaire radical: on the contrary, he was as opposed to Communism as was Robert Taft himself, and found in American society the highest attainment of the civil social order. Yet he was an egalitarian of sorts, in part a disciple of John Dewey, a fervent democrat and Democrat. One might have thought Taft imprudent to match himself against so lively an antagonist. These two were to discuss, in thirteen exchanges, such subjects as Congress, the Executive, the courts, the states, unemployment, social security, labor relations, foreign relations, agricultural policy, thrift or spending, and the future course of America. When the series commenced, Taft had been a senator less than two months.

To the surprise of many listeners, Taft had the better of the controversy. He was well prepared, as always; direct and sincere; and, by the brevity of the time allotted, compelled to be succinct. The orderliness of his lawyer's intellect stood him in good stead. On the other hand, T. V. Smith—usually a man of eloquence and grace—occasionally fell into a purple passage that did not much please the audience. (Smith's popularity as a platform speaker, too, depended in part upon his winning platform manner—not visible to a radio audience.)

Dispassionate though his voice was, Robert Taft's lucidity and practicality won for him this series of debates. A Gallup poll disclosed that some two-thirds of those who listened concluded that "Taft had the best argument." A writer for the radical *Nation* felt compelled to acknowledge that Taft "had whipped a prime New Deal intellectual, Representative T. V. Smith."[9] And Professor Smith, when the debates were done, generously remarked, "If the country has to suffer a Republican President, my hope is that it will be Mr. Taft."

Even though no one is likely to rank these brief talks of Taft with the major writings of American politics, the Taft half of *Foundations of Democracy* retains some enduring interest. "The American way of life," he began, "certainly does not guarantee equality in mental power or in character or in energy. It has only guaranteed that a man who had the necessary qualities might rise in public life and acquire a greater influence, a greater fame, a greater power, than his fellows; that he might rise in material wealth and acquire a greater comfort and luxury, if he desires it, for himself and his family; that he might earn a simple living on which he could base the development of true happiness for himself and his family without either wealth or power."

In his talk on Congress, Senator Taft incidentally referred to his dislike of political abstraction: "My picture of a statesman has always been a large, rather pompous gentleman, with his hand stuck into his coat, insisting on great principles which have little to do with everyday life." He proceeded, nevertheless, to give a description of Congress worthy of a true statesman, in the higher sense of that word.

The discussion of "The States—Sovereign or Subsidiary?" revealed that at one time Taft had not been the defender of the powers of state and local governments that he was during his public career: "When I started out in politics I was strong for centralization, on the theory that it would produce greater efficiency. The longer I have been in politics, the more I have come to doubt the premise of this conclusion. I doubt if centralized government is more efficient, certainly when it is centralized on a unit even as large as a state. I doubt whether efficiency is as important as an activity approved by the people who are being governed. . . . Their protests are listened to with consideration and care, and they have an opportunity within a reasonable time to replace those officials who do not give that consideration.

"How different conditions are in Washington! If you have ever come to Washington with a delegation on any subject, you must have felt that you came as suppliants, begging for action as a favor. There are ways to influence the action of the Washington Government through great national associations claiming to represent manufacturers or farmers or laborers, but within these organizations the individual members again have little influence. . . . The people themselves have a difficult time to obtain a hearing in Washington."

Taft's contributions to the debate contain remarks on the Wagner Act and on foreign policy which foreshadow his later endeavors in those fields. All in all, Taft made the clearest brief for the American conservative interest and for his party which had appeared since the first triumph of Franklin Roosevelt. Although *Foundations of Democracy* obtained nothing like the circulation of Senator Barry Goldwater's little book *Conscience of a Conservative*, more than twenty years later, it helped to establish Taft as the most thoughtful Republican in Congress. He concluded his talks with a passage which suggests the character of his whole long opposition to New Deal and Fair Deal:

"Unlike Representative Smith, many of the New Dealers have no concern whatever for individual freedom. They are collectivists, like Marx and Lenin and Mussolini. They believe in planned economy; that the Government should regulate every detail of industrial and commercial and agricultural life. They are willing to sacrifice individual freedom in order supposedly to improve the conditions of the poor and increase their material welfare. But in this purpose the policy has completely failed. . . . If any policy leans backward and not forward, it is the policy of spending billions of borrowed money and piling up a tremendous debt for future generations to pay. A policy which inevitably leads to bankruptcy and inflation of the currency will not only make the poor people poorer but it is likely to force a socialism which will utterly deprive them of individual freedom."[10]

A Reputation for Probity

Very early in his first senatorial term, then, Robert Taft had become the intellectual and moral chief of his party. He had been in Washington only a few months when many Republican organizations throughout the country commenced to smile upon him for the Republican presidential nomination of 1940. Support for his candidacy appeared to be quite as strong as that behind Governor Dewey's. Yet abruptly there emerged a rival who was to sweep aside, at the Convention, both Taft and Dewey—Wendell Willkie. Something very similar was to happen to Taft at the conventions of 1948 and 1952—although those curious events cannot be discussed in any detail in this book.

The New Dealers recognized Taft's ability, honesty, and devotion to the American republic quite as readily as did the Republicans, hard though Taft was upon Roosevelt's administration; and they saw that he could be trusted to defend the foundations of democracy. Harold Ickes, Secretary of the Interior when Taft came to the Senate, in his caustic way much preferred Taft over Dewey and Willkie, if some Republican must win the presidency. Knowing Taft's genuine abhorrence of arbitrary power, Ickes wrote in his secret diary that should it be necessary or expedient for the New Dealers to relinquish executive authority for a time, "if we could see more clearly ahead and could be certain that a man like Vandenberg or Taft, who would fight for our institutions, would be nominated, then it might be better for a conservative Republican to win in 1940."[11] Such men he considered more democratic and more truly liberal than Dewey or Willkie.

Of Dewey, Ickes recorded bitingly, "A person like Dewey, in command of a greatly augmented and improved Army and Navy, and with the power of concentrated wealth behind him, might do unpredictable things to our institutions, even in the short space of four years." He was more suspicious still of Willkie: "With him in the White House, the monied interests would be in full control and we could expect the American brand of fascism as soon as he could set it up."[12]

However fanciful a notion of Willkie's and Dewey's designs Harold Ickes may have entertained, he saw well enough that Taft could be trusted to maintain the American political system—and that Taft was always his own master. In his several attempts to obtain the Republican presidential nomination, Robert Taft never had the really "big money" at his back.

So much for Taft's emergence into national politics. The rest of this book will have to do with his principles of government and economics, as applied to the circumstances of his time. From first to last, without coherent support from "the monied interests" or any other powerful bloc, Taft dominated Congress and contended by force of mind and fortitude of soul against "the wave of the future." Thus we see him, near his end, in Duncan Norton-Taylor's sketch of Taft in the Eighty-Third Congress:

"Early in June he surrendered to his illness and gave up the position of majority leader. But wan and owl-like, hunched on crutches, he continued to attend committees, answer roll-calls, and exercise his power. . . . What was observable was Taft's unique position during those five months—a rejected candidate for the presidency, holding the Senate by the slender margin of one vote and with the hard core of his support no more than a dozen men who belonged to a so-called 'Taft faction' to which he himself did not properly belong. . . . This tall figure could be discerned walking behind every piece of legislation on the Hill."[13]

No other man of his age did so much as Robert Taft to shore up the fabric of representative government in America, "the foundations of democracy." Fourteen years after his death, this practical champion of principle, this adversary of fanatic ideology, still deserves the close attention of anyone seriously interested in the American political mind and in the functioning of American institutions.

Notes, CHAPTER II

1. Donald Davidson, *The Tennessee: the New River* (New York, 1948), pp. 243–244.

2. Jonathan Mitchell, "Taft: Unreconstructed Puritan," *The New Republic*, Vol. 102, No. 23 (June 3, 1949), p. 757.

3. James MacGregor Burns, *The Deadlock of Democracy* (Englewood Cliffs, N.J., 1963), p. 180.

4. Robert A. Taft, "A Republican Program," speech before the Republican Party Convention of Ohio, September 14, 1938. Copy in Robert A. Taft Papers, Library of Congress.

5. Arthur M. Schlesinger, Jr., "His Eyes Have Seen the Glory," *Collier's Magazine*, Vol. 119, No. 8 (February 22, 1947), p. 13.

6. Richard Rovere, "Taft: Is this the Best We've Got?," *Harper's Magazine*, Vol. 196, No. 1175 (April, 1948), p. 289.

7. Joseph and Stewart Alsop, "Taft and Vandenberg," *Life*, Vol. 21, No. 15 (October 7, 1946), p. 103.

8. Willard Shelton, "Portrait of a Conservative," *New Republic*, Vol. 120, No. 14 (April 4, 1949), p. 18.

9. Willard Shelton, "The Retrogression of Senator Taft," *The Nation*, Vol. 174, No. 20 (May 17, 1952), p. 473.

10. T. V. Smith and Robert A. Taft, *Foundations of Democracy: a Series of Debates* (New York, 1939).

11. Harold L. Ickes, *The Secret Diary*, Vol. III, *The Lowering Clouds* (New York, 1955), p. 102.

12. *Ibid.*, p. 212.

13. Duncan Norton-Taylor, "Robert Taft's Congress," *Fortune*, Vol. XLVII, No. 2 (August, 1953), pp. 136, 138.

CHAPTER III

The Struggle for Responsible Party

Statesmanship through Partisanship

COHERENT POLITICAL PARTIES of the modern sort began to develop—in Britain, first of all—during the last quarter of the eighteenth century. If parties were lacking, true representative government would be impossible, and democracy on a national scale would be a sham. Precisely because Robert Taft was devoted to the American republic, and because he sought to protect and advance the general national interest, he was a firm partisan.

This chapter is an endeavor to outline Taft's work for responsible party in the United States. He found the Republican party feeble and confused; he labored to define its principles and to convert it into a coherent opposition to the party which dominated the executive branch of the general government until the last months of his life; he hoped to restore that tension between two great parties which has been one of the healthier characteristics of political existence in the United States, Britain, and some other modern powers.

Of course he was not wholly successful. Ever since 1932 (except for the first two years of Eisenhower's presidency) the Republican party, nationally considered, has been conspicuously weaker than the Democratic, less firmly led, and sometimes uncertain of its own reasons for existence. That

Taft himself, despite his intellectual ascendancy and his long services to his party, was thrice denied that party's presidential nomination is considerable evidence of the Republicans' vacillation and hankering after office (as set against adherence to a body of political principles and general aspirations).

Yet Taft restored to the Republicans some measure of responsibility; through his party (sometimes in coalition with Democratic factions) he repeatedly set limits to the action of the national executive and the majority party; and he saved the Republicans from sinking to the condition of a mere faction of negation. The end of his influence as a party leader is not yet.

In modern society, the alternatives to government through responsible parties are unpleasant: tyranny, oligarchy, "plebiscitary democracy" (a domination growing in power, in much of the world, during Taft's time), or anarchy. These alternatives were not, and are not, inconceivable in the United States. So to reproach Taft for standing steadfastly with his party is to reproach him for his attachment to ordered freedom. "Nonpartisanship" and "bipartisanship," as general modes of operation, practically are impossible in a vast democratic republic. Only by lifting party above simple passion for office and patronage, above demagoguery and time-serving, can justice and the national interest be secured. Such was Taft's aspiration, and it ran through everything he did and said concerning domestic or foreign policy.

A Party in the Wilderness

Robert Taft was one of six new Republican senators elected in 1938. Franklin Roosevelt's attempt to pull America out of the Depression through radical improvisations had been unsuccessful, for the most part. Despite all the funds expended upon "pump priming" and public relief, despite assistance to industry, labor, and agriculture, despite alteration of the constitutional pattern and mighty expansion of governmental activities to accomplish these measures, the hard fact remained that by 1939 the United States continued in an economic depression. Positive want had been notably diminished; but the New Deal was not functioning as its authors had hoped, and public discontent was strong.

In Congress, if one counts both Republicans and those Democrats often in opposition to Roosevelt, the critics of the New Deal and the Fair Deal usually outnumbered the advocates of Roosevelt's and Truman's programs, from 1939 to 1948. As Samuel Lubell remarks, "Roosevelt's winning a third and a fourth term has obscured the fact that the last major measure of a New Deal nature which he was able to get through Congress was the Wages and Hours Law in mid-1938."[1]

In addition to gaining six seats in the Senate, in 1938 the Republicans had won eighty more seats in the House of Representatives. In effect, the New Deal had run its course by the time Taft arrived in Washington, even though the President wished to push forward. The grand experiment was terminated by powerful men in the Democratic party itself, working with the Republican minority in Congress.

"I am learning the ropes," Taft wrote to his old friend Herbert Hoover, shortly after taking his senatorial seat. "The Republicans are still in a small minority, but I doubt very much if the President could get anything extreme through the present Senate."[2] A few weeks later, he wrote to Horace Taft, "There is not much interesting about the Senate. . . . We move very slowly, but I get the distinct impression that the New Deal is on the defensive, and that their representatives in Congress are not very hopeful about their ability to defend it successfully."[3]

He was right. The New Deal did not expire merely of inanition; it had been rejected in considerable part by Congress and the public before Taft entered the Senate, and got almost nowhere after 1938. And yet for the following thirteen years, Taft found it necessary to argue incessantly with leading members of his own party as to whether the Republicans should come to terms with the allegedly triumphant New Deal. Many Republicans continued in a political trauma, shocked by their defeats of 1932 and 1936, and could think only of making concessions to the new order, rather than presenting feasible alternatives to Franklin Roosevelt's proposals. Just such timidity led to the nominations of Willkie and Dewey, and Taft never wholly dispelled this Celtic Twilight mood of the Republicans, who in election after election behaved like men expected to fight, but never to conquer.

This Republican mood is not difficult to explain. In 1936, the Republican presidential candidate had carried only Maine and Vermont; by that same national election, the number of Republicans in the House had been reduced from one hundred and three to eighty-nine, and in the Senate from twenty-five to seventeen. With this overwhelming defeat only four years after the catastrophic reverse of 1932, a good many serious observers believed that the Republicans would follow the Whigs and the Federalists down to dusty death. The victory of 1938 was heartening—yet not sufficient to convince Republicans generally that Roosevelt and the New Deal were in retreat. They did not altogether understand that Congress's rejection of Roosevelt's plan for "packing" the Supreme Court had been a sea-wall erected against domestic innovation—indeed, against the whole revolutionary character of the New Deal—and that thereafter the tide of constitutional change would ebb. It was primarily conservative Democratic opposition, rather than Republican, which had told Franklin Roosevelt he must go no farther.

During Taft's years in the Senate, the Republicans continued to increase in numbers. Between 1940 and 1944, they gained twenty-one seats in the House and fifteen in the Senate. In 1946, with a campaign slogan of "Had Enough?," they obtained fifty-six more seats in the House and thirteen in the Senate, becoming the Congressional majority for the first time since 1928: the Eightieth Congress, led by Senators Taft and Vandenberg, represented a powerful Republican revival.

And yet though the New Deal was waning, Republican

national conventions continued to nominate liberal candidates for the presidency—all, in turn, defeated—while the conservative Congressional Republicans steadily increased their strength. It is not surprising that Senator Taft regarded what is called the "me too" stand of the liberal Republicans as a formula for political failure.

The Republican party, it now seems clear, had not closely examined its own prospects in 1939, and in some measure has not yet looked sufficiently into its own principles and possibilities. During the first seven years of Franklin Roosevelt's ascendancy, the theories and implications of the New Deal never had been adequately criticized by the battered Republican opposition. Robert Taft set to work supplying that vigorous critical examination.

He was deeply disquieted by the temperament and the mentality of the men around Franklin Roosevelt. Had it been in their power, many of Roosevelt's principal advisers would have gone immensely further, during the first seven years of the New Deal, than Congress and the public desired. They participated in the climate of opinion dominating most of the world in those years: they put their faith in the formulas of collectivism.

And Roosevelt, with some doubts and reservations, had listened to them. In his Commonwealth Club speech (written by Adolph A. Berle and Rexford Guy Tugwell) during his first presidential campaign, Roosevelt had declared that "equality of opportunity . . . no longer exists"; it must be supplanted by a new plan, the government guaranteeing equality of prospects and a standard of living, rather than merely opening the way to individual opportunities. The time had come, Roosevelt had proclaimed, for the federal government to create a new society in which "prosperity is uniform [and] purchasing power is well distributed throughout every group in the nation."[4]

Yet by comparison with the ambitions of many New Dealers, these views were moderate. Professor Lewis S. Feuer carefully describes the influence of the Soviet Union's example upon many of those Americans who shaped, directly or at some remove, the New Deal:

> The whole conception of a "social experiment," the whole notion of planned human intervention in social processes to raise the welfare of the people, had become linked in the minds of America's intellectual and social leaders with the practice of the Soviet Union. This transformation in American thought was largely the work of a small number of several hundreds of travellers to the Soviet Union during the previous decade. If there was no de Tocqueville among them, the reports which they published affected the American political consciousness more deeply nonetheless than any other foreign influence in its history.[5]

John Dewey, revered by so many of the New Dealers, in 1928 had written for the *New Republic* a series of articles about his impressions of Soviet Russia. Of that totalist domination, he had declared that "The main effort is nobly heroic, evincing a faith in human nature which is democratic beyond the ambitions of the democracies of the past."[6] Like others, Dewey was to change his mind somewhat later; but meanwhile Dewey's admirers and colleagues were making public policy in America.

Dr. Feur gives a detailed account of how such New Dealers—thinkers, officials, publicists—as R. G. Tugwell, Paul Douglas, Stuart Chase (who coined the term "New Deal"), Harry Hopkins, E. C. Lindemann, Bruce Bliven, Oswald Garrison Villard, and Henry Wallace heaped praise upon the Soviet Union. And he remarks:

> To what extent finally did the reports of the American travellers to the Soviet Union affect the political philosophy of Franklin D. Roosevelt? From the first, Roosevelt had a sympathetic interest in the Soviet effort at social reconstruction, and regarded its experimentalism and social idealism as akin to his own. . . . Early in his administration, on October 5, 1933, President Roosevelt told his Secretary of the Interior, Harold L. Ickes, that "what we

are doing in this country were some of the things that were being done in Russia and even some of the things that were being done under Hitler in Germany. But we are doing them in an orderly way."[7]

Robert Taft had reason, then, for his conviction that American constitutions and American social establishments were not wholly secure under such a national administration. In their profound suspicion of the New Deal's motives and ideological passion, nearly all eminent Republicans were at one with Taft; yet not all Republican leaders were ready to take, by Taft's side, a forthright stand against the collectivistic assumptions upon which the New Deal had been erected. In part, before Taft arrived in the Senate, this Republican ineffectuality and ignorance of principle was produced by the lack of able Republicans inside Congress—a point touched upon at the time by Walter Lippmann, who remarked that the American political structure prevented the more penetrating critics of the New Deal from being heard in Congress (and so by the nation), thus producing "such spectacles as the attempt of Republican Senators to debate the money bill though they did not understand it, while Mr. Hoover and Mr. Ogden Mills, who have the equipment to understand it, are not heard in the debate."[8]

Taft did understand such matters; and once he arrived in the Senate, the Republican party in Congress was reinvigorated. That party throughout the country, nevertheless, was less easily quickened in its wits. Those regulars who hold a party together, in fat times and in lean, knew Taft's worth and worked for him; most of the Republican state chairmen, the great majority of county chairmen, the typical delegates to state conventions, the precinct workers, were "Taft men"—in part because Taft never neglected them. More than anyone else, Taft stood for what they believed, though they could not express half so logically as did Taft the convictions of the staunch Republican.

Yet it was otherwise with Taft's principal rivals for national party leadership, and often with a large part of that multitude vaguely attached to the Republican party which hoped to find some champion with Roosevelt's magnetism. Also, Taft's party influence was less strong in the populous northeastern states than elsewhere in the country; and an invincible suspicion of the soundness of the "Eastern crowd" of Republican politicians and party backers hung at the back of Taft's mind.

The "liberal," or anti-Taft, element of the Republican party (waxing or waning in strength, according to circumstance) acted upon the assumption that the New Deal was irrevocable. Concessions, therefore, must be made to public opinion, allegedly infatuated with Roosevelt's programs—large concessions, made with the best face possible; and presidential candidates must be secured whose personality and background would not remind the electorate overmuch that the Republican party's rank and file detested the assumptions of the New Deal. Victory at the polls, rather than the defense or vindication of principles, seemed to most of the liberal Republicans the object of their party. In some matters, it might be possible to outbid the New Dealers; in most, to offer nearly as much as Roosevelt offered. Hoover and Landon had fallen before a public repudiation of the old order; and the liberal Republicans assumed that the public's mood had not altered much since 1936, and would not alter. They accepted "the inevitability of gradualism," for the most part.

So the tactics of the three Republican candidates for the presidency during Taft's senatorial years were quite different from the assault on the premises of the New Deal and the Fair Deal which Taft directed from the Senate. For Willkie, Dewey, and Eisenhower, with their campaign managers and chief supporters, campaigned on the explicit or implicit ground that Republicans were better qualified to administer those national programs which the Democrats had happened to initiate. This amounted to a confession, perhaps, that the Democratic party was the party of initiative, of ideas, of new policies, of intellectual leadership. These rivals of Taft did not venture, very often, to challenge the basic assumptions of New Deal and Fair Deal. Accordingly, the Republican principles which Taft erected in Congress regularly fell into neglect during the heat of presidential campaigns.

Still, so far as any man might speak for Republicanism, that leader was Robert Taft, whose course in Congress helped to restore Republican confidence and to make possible some Republican alternative proposals, once the Democrats were divided among themselves, beginning in 1938. But the spreading of the Second World War interrupted the debate over New Deal measures, and Taft's own interests presently shifted to foreign affairs. With discussion of the New Deal virtually suspended, various of Roosevelt's programs became permanent; and when Roosevelt—or after him, Truman—felt it necessary to reply at all to criticisms of their domestic programs, usually they ignored the Republican presidential candidates, instead directing their replies to Taft, as a politician worthy of their steel.

Although nothing is deader than dead politics, and although the New Deal no longer is conspicuously controversial—being in part forgotten, in part abandoned, and in part now accepted by both parties—still Taft's endeavor to concert a responsible and imaginative Republican criticism of the New Deal deserves close attention. His own forcible objections to the New Deal's theories and practices never were adequately answered by Franklin Roosevelt and the men around him. As Richard Hofstadter observes, Roosevelt substantially abandoned domestic experiment after 1938: "What would have happened to the political fortunes of Franklin Roosevelt if the war had not created a new theater for his leadership?"[9] (If Roosevelt himself recognized that the New Deal no longer had popular enthusiasm behind it, still many Republican politicians continued to believe that their party could not successfully set itself against the New Deal's dogmas.)

Even today, the attitude of many Republicans toward the New Deal remains ambiguous. Some attention will be paid in the chapters of this book concerned with liberty, justice, and economic questions to Taft's criticism of the New Deal, nevertheless; for the theoretical basis of the New Deal, however modified and chastened by hard experience, remains a force in American politics.

Taft's Understanding of Party

In domestic or in foreign policy, Senator Taft labored under a heavy handicap when he tried to define Republican principles. For his party, before its defeats in 1930 and 1932, had been little more than the party of prosperity: with prosperity vanished, the Republicans were all at sea. This feebleness of party principles had not been peculiar to the Republicans, of course, nor to the era of the Great Depression. Bryce, writing in 1893, refers to the lack of discernible enduring principle in either Democratic or Republican party:

"Neither party has any clear-cut principles, any distinctive tenets. Both have traditions. Both claim to have tendencies. Both certainly have war cries, organizations, interests listed in their support. But those interests are in the main interests of getting or keeping the patronage of the government. . . . The American parties now continue to exist because they have existed. The mill has been constructed, and its machinery goes on turning even when there is no grist to grind."[10]

A Republican party of this character, however, could not stand successfully against a Democratic party which, at least during the first five years of the New Deal, had acquired a strong ideological cast. As a believer in responsible party, Taft feared, indeed, that the party system might give way to government by pressure groups, more determined than the old amorphous parties, unrelated to the old political constituencies, and alien to the American Constitution. "He was far more interested," as George H. Mayer writes, "in curtailing the power of pressure groups which had been nurtured by the New Deal than in indiscriminately repealing New Deal legislation."[11]

To resist interest groups, and to contend against the destructive power of ideology, Robert Taft endeavored to return his party to principle. His understanding of party was very like Edmund Burke's. The representative and his party, Burke had said in his address to the electors of Bristol, should not so much reflect the public opinion of the moment as they should represent, in a wider and more enduring sense, the "best judgment" of the electorate—the views which citizens would hold tomorrow. Burke elsewhere defined political party as "a body of men united for promoting, by their joint endeavors, the national interest, upon some particular principle, in which they are agreed."[12]

For Taft, as for Burke, the function of party was more than simply providing for an orderly transfer of power, or of merely consolidating public opinion. A political party must stand, as Burke said, upon the principles which brought it into being, even at the risk—or the certitude—of defeat at the polls. The party truly patriotic and responsible is the party more inclined to follow the public interest than the public passion; a party, indeed, which is more devoted to the national interest than to the immediate advantage of the party's stalwart members.

A leader of party, or even a lesser political representative, owes loyalty to his party—but not to his party alone, nor necessarily to the men who, for the moment, may have contrived to dominate that party. In the phrase of Santayana, "A party is not the whole people, and if a representative is bound to express only the will of his party he is not a fair representative of a truly self-governing people."[13]

The party which abides by principle must be willing to oppose the majority of voters, if need be, in defending those principles; it must be willing to go out of office, or to abstain from taking office, if the price of power is the sacrifice of that party's reason for existence. And the party's leaders must be ready, in time of need, to oppose elements of their own party when some abandon those principles and thereby harm the national interest.

"The political parties which I call great," Tocqueville wrote in *Democracy in America*, "are those which cling to principles rather than to their consequences, to general and not to special cases, to ideas and not to men."[14] As a champion of the American democracy of elevation and limitation that Tocqueville described, Taft struggled to revive a party of principles, general cases, and ideas.

For that matter, Franklin Roosevelt was by no means content with the Democratic party he had led to victory: his unsuccessful endeavor to "purge" the Democratic party of conservatives, just before Taft entered the Senate, was the consequence of his belief that "the Democratic Party and the Republican Party should not be Tweedledum and Tweedledee to each other." One party should be liberal and the other conservative, Roosevelt argued: "This has been the division by which the major parties in American history have identified themselves whenever crises have developed which require a definite choice of direction. . . . A nation can never intelligently determine its policy, if it has to go through the confusion of voting for candidates who pretend to be one thing but who act the other. . . . I have always believed, and I have frequently stated, that my own party can succeed at the polls only so long as it continues to be the party of militant liberalism."[15] Later, in 1944, Roosevelt was to propose to Wendell Willkie (who had lost the Republican presidential nomination) that he and Willkie should unite to form a new, "really liberal party."[16]

But Senator Taft did not desire to convert the major American parties into ideological factions, with all the rigidity and intolerance that accompany the binding of party to abstract doctrine and theoretic dogma. On the one hand, he abjured a vulgar "pragmatism" which took no long views; on the other, he repelled the fanatic clutch of ideology. Though he was, as he described himself, a liberal conservative, he did not mean to create a Conservative party founded upon inflexible doctrine and class interest. (In the last year of Taft's life, a journalist asked him if he had read Russell Kirk's book *The Conservative Mind*, published a few months before. "He shook his head and chuckled: 'You remind me of Thurber's

Let Your Mind Alone.' " His implication was that he had been
too active *being* a conservative to read about the subject.)*

And Taft rejected the argument of many commentators
(whether hostile or friendly toward the existing party structure) that present institutional factors prevent parties from
abiding by principles, and that only vast alteration of party
structure, or of the American constitutional system, could
make possible principled parties. He believed that his party
already stood, however confusedly, for a genuine body of
interest and opinion. He was not creating a new party as an act
of political genius, but restoring an old one. The party's
principles must reflect the convictions of the party's membership. "The principles of a great party," he declared, "are not
made by its leaders, nor by the National Committee, nor by
Congress itself, but by the great bulk of party members
throughout the country."

He denied that sectional, economic, and ethnic differences
among its members made it impossible for a party to stand on
general principles; he argued that such differences may be
surmounted: "The two-party system is based on the theory
that a large number of men who think differently on many
subjects unite in the belief that certain principles are vital to
the welfare of their country, and that differences on less
important questions must be reconciled or forgotten in the
common effort to secure those basic principles. . . . The only
parties that have died are those that have forgotten or abandoned the principle on which they were founded. A party can
live only if it represents a great principle or a set of principles."[17] On another occasion, he had said hotly that "a party
kills itself and removes any excuse for its existence when it
adopts the principles of its opponents."[18]

Taft saw that both the disregard for political principles and
the dilemma of the Republican party at the polls were caused
by the American people's lack of understanding of their
political patrimony. The Republican party, he maintained,

* Duncan Norton-Taylor, "Robert Taft's Congress," *Fortune*, Vol.
XLVIII, No. 2 (August, 1953), p. 145.

must offer the people a reasoned defense of the American heritage; and its principles must reflect love of American traditions.

So the type of party reform which Taft proposed was didactic. The task for the Republican party, he affirmed, was to educate the American electorate, schooling the voters in Republican principles. An uninformed public was the grimmest obstacle to a Republican revival. He was quite aware how formidable an undertaking this must be, and raised the subject in a speech to the alumni of Yale, in 1947:

> The American people seem to be doing less and less thinking for themselves and they seem to have less and less knowledge of the history and basic principles of the American Republic. . . . It seems to me that the people have come to form their opinions, not from facts and their own thinking, but from the thinking and opinions of others. Perhaps it is due to the development of motion pictures and radio. To listen to either requires only the slightest mental effort. They are a kind of education or recreation which gives knowledge without thought. . . . The truth is that there is hardly one [commentator or columnist] who has not a strong bias for one philosophy or another, for one party or another, for one man or another. This they attempt to conceal, and the unthinking are likely to take them at their own estimate of their impartiality. . . . The radio is a peculiarly plausible instrument, more so than the written word. . . . But even the news today in many newspapers is given a strong slant in the direction of the paper's policy. . . . Public opinion is formed without any real knowledge or analysis of the facts of the issues. . . .
>
> No one today seems to be interested in facts . . . or the teaching of the fundamentals of American government. It is a task which has been poorly performed for many years throughout the United States. . . . Today, according to a recent poll, only 17 per cent of the people know what the Bill of Rights is. Only a small percentage understand the principles of the Constitution and the

functions of the state and local governments. Only a limited number realize that the true purpose of this country was to achieve freedom of thought, freedom of government, and freedom of opportunity. . . .

Today the interest of the people has come to center entirely in the field of economics . . . and the material welfare of the citizens. Programs are judged on the question of whether they give men more money, more bathtubs, more automobiles, and less time to work. Certainly no one can be against these economic objectives, but it is wrong to subordinate to them the need for greater morality, greater liberty of thought, and greater liberty of action. I believe that opportunity and not security is still the goal of the American people if they think about it.[19]

Despite these difficulties, Taft did not lose hope for the reform of party through the education of the electorate. "The defeats of the Republican Party," he wrote in an article published in *Fortune*, "have not been due to its principles, but to its failure to present those principles effectively to the people. They are not principles that interpret themselves easily. . . . The Republican Party will continue to live and will take over the administration of government if it dedicates itself again to the principles for which it was founded, and if it presents those principles in the most forceful and effective manner, not only in elections but at all times."[20]

Precisely what were the principles which Taft meant to restore and present afresh? In detail, those concepts are discussed in the succeeding chapters of this book. But fundamentally, Taft said, "I believe that the only object of government is to serve the people and help them become a greater people in the best sense. We want a better people, people of a strong character—God-fearing, industrious, self-reliant, honorable and intelligent. I think almost too much emphasis has been laid on material well-being, or the so-called standard of living, and on plumbing. A very high standard of living is not essential for these purposes."[21] Elsewhere, he wrote that the Republicans must stand for liberty, prosperity, "the prevention of hardship and poverty," equal justice under law, "equality without special privileges," and peace.[22]

Thus he stood almost at the political antipodes—at least in his interpretation of these objectives—from Tugwell, Berle, Wallace, Hopkins, and the other ideologues of the New Deal. In and out of the Senate, he spoke over and over again on the subjects of individual liberty, the encouragement and protection of a free economy, and the forming of a foreign policy that would maintain the peace without sacrificing the national interest. But would his Republican party fight its elections on such principles?

The Republican Dilemma

The Republican party's dilemma, says Samuel Lubell, "has been the necessity of choosing between embracing or repudiating the conservative coalition in Congress."[23] That has been true of Republican presidential choices—and campaign platforms, in presidential years—ever since the defeat of Herbert Hoover. The "conservative coalition" has meant the vigorous Republican opposition of which Taft was the best representative, loosely allied in Congress, on some issues, with conservative Democrats. The alternative has been a candidate of "moderate" or "middle-of-the-road" reputation (and, preferably, of winning personality) with a platform of compromise, concession, and liberal generalities. Except for the Republican nomination of Barry Goldwater, in 1964, Republican national conventions have chosen candidates and platforms of the latter description. These choices also have been dictated by expediency over principle.

In the enormous democracies of the twentieth century, the conflicting claims of pressure groups frequently master the public man, to the exclusion of concern for basic principles of party. Thus the party founded on principle is at a disadvantage, except perhaps in times of crisis: for trying to mediate the differences of interest groups on a basis of principle may be denounced as "undemocratic"—and it may seem impractical, since the dissatisfied pressure group may shift its power to an opposing party. Such considerations were in the forefront of the minds of Republican leaders who, strong though their preference for Taft's forthright politics might be, decided to nominate some candidate outside the "conservative coalition" in Congress.

Except in the instance of General Eisenhower, this evading of a direct clash on first principles with the dominant Democratic politicians was not rewarded by Republican success. The Republican platform upon which Alfred Landon campaigned, in 1936, "concealed the abandonment of traditional positions behind a smoke-screen of rhetoric," writes the most recent historian of the Republican party. "The underlying theme was one of capitulation to a new order."[24] To the astonishment of some people, Landon was beaten worse than Hoover had been.

Wendell Willkie, unknown to most Republican leaders until shortly before the convention of 1940, agreed with Roosevelt in much, and promised chiefly that he would administer the national government more efficiently. He was able to take only ten states in the election; and though the Republicans gained five Senate seats in that year, they lost seven in the House.

In 1944 and 1948, Thomas E. Dewey, a liberal Republican, was little more willing or able than Willkie had been to stand on such principles as Robert Taft had enunciated. Although Roosevelt's popularity was declining in 1944, that was not enough to put a temporizing Republican in the White House; and in 1948, Dewey accomplished the remarkable feat of contriving to be beaten by President Truman, whose reputation had been at its nadir until the campaign commenced.

Even the thumping victory of Dwight Eisenhower, in 1952, after three decades of Republican adversity, was almost wholly the personal success of a popular military commander.

The Republican party steadily declined while Eisenhower held office—declined in Congress, and in state and local elections. The Republicans lost their Congressional majorities in 1954, being deprived of one seat in the Senate and eighteen in the House. When Eisenhower was re-elected in 1956, the Republicans merely held their own in the Senate, and lost two more seats in the House. In the Congressional elections of 1958, the Republicans lost forty-seven House seats and thirteen Senate seats. Just how pronounced a decline this was, despite the personal appeal of Eisenhower, may be suggested by the fact that in the years 1938, 1940, 1942, 1944, 1946, 1948, and 1950, there were more Republican representatives in the House than there remained in 1958; while in 1938, 1942, 1944, 1948, and 1950, there were more Republican senators than in 1958. When President Eisenhower retired from office in 1960, the Republican party was as impotent as it had been in the darkest days of the Great Depression.

Richard Nixon, indeed, obtained some sort of consensus within the Republican party during his presidential candidacy in 1960; yet it was at the expense of clarity and forcefulness. This vagueness, combining with a curious chain of small historical accidents, was sufficient to account for more than the fraction of one per cent of the popular vote by which Nixon lost the election.*

On the other hand, the Republicans were badly defeated when their national convention, in 1964, embraced the doctrines of Senator Goldwater and the party leadership em-

---

* Theodore White, comparing the Democratic and Republican party principles in the light of the 1960 presidential election, makes this perceptive comment: "The Republican philosophy is entirely different, clearer in metaphysical terms yet murkier in political expression. It is the belief, deep down, that each citizen bears a responsibility in private life and in community life as great or greater than the responsibility of government to shape that life and community. Part of the Republican tragedy in recent years has been the inability of its thinkers to articulate this philosophy clearly enough to draw political conclusions and programs from it." (White, *The Making of a President, 1960* [New York, 1961], p. 363.)

barked upon a campaign which appealed almost exclusively to the conservative interest. Neither the Republican liberals nor the Republican conservatives achieved that unity and integrity of party which Robert Taft had sought.

Particular parties may disappear, and yet the republic may endure. But the prolonged domination of one invincible party, unchecked by a sanguine opposition, is a graver matter. In such circumstances, government is dominated by factions and pressure groups, many of these virtually unrecognized by the public, and little influenced by the constitutional structure of the commonwealth. Those individuals and interests not enjoying the favor of the dominant factions and pressure groups become virtually defenseless, and may be despoiled, unchampioned by a vigilant opposition party; and in the long run, the national welfare suffers proportionately—a point repeatedly emphasized by Robert Taft.

The final defeat of Taft for his party's presidential nomination appears, in historical perspective, to have been a rout of the essential Republican party—though not necessarily a permanent fall. Taft's admirers—who were numerous and ardent, despite Taft's disdain for the techniques of mass public relations—sank into despair. "Yes, Bob is gone and there is no one to take his place," wrote the publisher of the New Bedford *Standard-Times*, on the day Taft died. "This alone is a tragedy comparable to the passing of Lincoln. But with Bob Taft goes the Republican Party. In its place is a faceless, slinking thing, bearing only the name Republican, a name indeed which President Eisenhower hardly has mentioned since he was elected under its label."[25]

Yet Taft himself would not have had a party dependent upon the existence of a single politician. Though men pass, principles last; and sometimes a party which repairs to its old principles enjoys a second vigor.

Writing in the period of Republican hegemony, Lord Bryce explained why "great men are not chosen President" of the United States. "The ordinary American voter," he remarked, "does not object to mediocrity. He has a lower conception of the qualities requisite to make a statesman than those who direct public opinion in Europe have. He likes his candidate to be sensible, vigorous, and, above all, what he calls 'magnetic,' and does not value, because he sees no need for originality or profundity, a fine culture or a wide range of knowledge."[26]

Robert Taft was not magnetic; but nothing about him was mediocre. He, of all leading Republicans, was fertile in ideas. His rejection as presidential candidate was a rejection not of "Neanderthal" Republicanism, but a rejection of intelligent principle. It was not even a question, really, of "liberalism" against "conservatism" (in the journalistic sense of those terms) within the Republican party: for in such matters of social reform as governmental activity in the fields of public housing, education, and health, Taft was more imaginatively liberal than most of the "liberal" Republicans who were his opponents within the party.

Taft's inability to ascend to the presidency certainly is not unique in American political history: parties often have chosen not to nominate their most able men, preferring magnetism or mediocrity. But the reluctance of Taft's party to support wholeheartedly, at the time of presidential elections, the principles which Taft defined and in which, really, the great majority of Republicans believed—that is a graver matter.

An irresponsible party is a curse, not merely for the things it does, but because it fails to check entrenched power competently, and because it pre-empts the ground which some more responsible and vigorous party otherwise might occupy. "Strong government," comments a recent English critic of American political science and practice, "needs strong opposition if it is to be free and effective government."[27]

Having gained nothing by endeavoring to ignore Taft's principles, even Republican liberals might profit, tardily, from examining what Taft actually said and believed. For that matter, Americans of any political persuasion are likely to benefit by some review of the ideas of a remarkably able man who gave himself up to party—with little relish, at bottom, for the painful task—that he might maintain the republic.

Notes, CHAPTER III

1. Samuel Lubell, *The Future of American Politics* (New York, 1956), p. 13.
2. Robert Taft to Herbert Hoover, January 23, 1939. Copy in Robert A. Taft Papers, Library of Congress.
3. Robert Taft to Horace Taft, March 9, 1939. Copy in Robert A. Taft Papers, Library of Congress.
4. *Public Papers of Franklin D. Roosevelt*, Vol. I (New York, 1938), pp. 750–752.
5. Lewis S. Feuer, "Travelers to the Soviet Union, 1917–1932: the Formation of a Component of New Deal Ideology," *American Quarterly*, Vol. XIV, No. 2, Part 1 (summer, 1962).
6. John Dewey's praise of the Soviet Union in the pages of the *New Republic* is reprinted in his *Characters and Events*, edited by Joseph Ratner (New York, 1929), and in his *Impressions of Soviet Russia and the Revolutionary World* (New York, 1932).
7. *The Secret Diary of Harold L. Ickes*, Vol. I, *The First Thousand Days* (New York, 1953), p. 104.
8. Quoted in E. E. Robinson, *The Roosevelt Leadership* (New York, 1964), p. 483.
9. Richard Hofstadter, *The American Political Tradition and the Men Who Made It* (New York, 1948), p. 338.
10. James Bryce, *The American Commonwealth*, Vol. II (New York, 1911), pp. 21, 24.
11. George H. Mayer, *The Republican Party, 1854–1964* (New York, 1964), p. 483.
12. Edmund Burke, *Thoughts on the Present Discontents* (1770). The best-annotated edition is that of E. J. Payne, *Edmund Burke, Select Works*, Vol. I (London, 1904).
13. George Santayana, *Dominations and Powers* (New York, 1954), p. 383.
14. Alexis de Tocqueville, *Democracy in America* (edited by Phillips Bradley, New York, 1948), Vol. I, p. 175.

15. *Public Papers of Franklin Roosevelt*, Vol. 7 (New York, 1941), pp. xxii–xxxi.

16. As related by James MacGregor Burns, "Republicans, Democrats: Who's Who?," *New York Times Magazine*, January 2, 1955, p. 42.

17. Robert A. Taft, "The Republican Party," *Fortune*, Vol. XXXIX, No. 4 (April 1949), p. 108. This article is a revision of a speech delivered by Taft at the McKinley Memorial at Niles, Ohio, on January 28, 1949, and printed in the *Congressional Record*, 81st Congress, 1st Session, Vol. 94, Part 12, pp. A447–449.

18. Robert A. Taft, speech to the American Irish Historical Society, New York, May 2, 1942; printed in the *Congressional Record*, 77th Congress, 2nd Session, Vol. 88, Part 9, p. A1622.

19. Robert A. Taft, speech to the Yale Alumni, February 22, 1947, at New Haven; printed in the *Congressional Record*, 80th Congress, 1st Session, Vol. 93, Part 10, pp. A793–794.

20. Robert A. Taft, "The Republican Party," in *Fortune, op. cit.*, pp. 108–109.

21. As quoted in Caroline Thomas Harnsberger, *A Man of Courage* (Chicago, 1952), p. 133.

22. Robert A. Taft, "The Republican Party," *op. cit.*, pp. 109 ff.

23. Samuel Lubell, *The Future of American Politics, op. cit.*, p. 248.

24. Mayer, *The Republican Party, op. cit.*, p. 440.

25. Quoted in Malcolm Moos, *The Republicans: A History of their Party* (New York, 1956), p. 482.

26. Bryce, *The American Commonwealth*, Vol. I, *op. cit.*, p. 79.

27. Bernard Crick, *In Defense of Politics* (Chicago, 1962), p. 66.

CHAPTER IV

Liberty Under Law

The Shadow of the Total State

"IN SEEKING A GUIDING PRINCIPLE," said Senator Taft, in the last year of his life, "I have come more and more to believe that the consideration which ought to determine almost every decision of policy today is the necessity of preserving, maintaining, and increasing the liberty of the people of our country, as fundamental to every other progressive purpose. Every policy should be tested on that touchstone, whether it increases or decreases the liberty of our people and the promise of continued liberty in the future."[1]

By the time Robert Taft was elected to Congress, the New Dealers' admiration for the Soviet experiment had diminished markedly; yet there remained the possibility that the United States might slide, almost unwittingly, toward totalist politics. The maintenance of ordered freedom being the root of Taft's politics, he never ceased to warn the American public against the erosion of constitutional principles; and he never was deterred by ridicule.

"The trend of thought on forms of government throughout the entire world," Taft insisted, "has been pushing all peoples consciously or unconsciously away from democracy to different forms of totalitarianism. In Europe, democratic ideals were crushed between the dynamic dogmas of Communism and

62

Fascism. In the United States, we often lose sight of the real nature of the principles on which freedom depends, in our desire to remake our world according to the popular method of the day—methods formulated for the most part by European socialists."[2] The American people had perceived by 1938, he said, that this tendency was most perilous; but the coming of the war had diverted public attention from such fundamental concerns.[3]

So in speech upon speech, during the Second World War, Taft prodded Americans into vigilance against the encroachment of collectivistic ideas and measures at home. Some of the basic principles of American politics already had been damaged, he declared in 1941: "We have seen during the past twelve years a steady increase in government regulation of business and of the individual, and we have seen, through courts which are hardly independent of the executive, a constant tendency to increase the powers of the Federal government over the states, and the powers of the Executive over the individual."[4]

He was contending against the grim drift of the mass age, in which freedom may be lost in a fit of absence of mind. One cannot call his earnest speeches a rousing summons to arms against the total state; for Taft had no touch of fancy, and (very unlike Franklin Roosevelt) he laboriously wrote his own speeches. But his audiences understood that he meant every word he uttered. To those who do not recall the appetite of many New Dealers for grandiose designs, nor the passionate eagerness of men like Harry Hopkins to use the war as pretext for permanent direction of many things by the central government, his words may seem exaggerated. But in part that is because Taft, and men of his mind in either party, succeeded in terminating the emergency powers of government when the war was done—succeeded not without difficulty.

Perhaps the best expression of his views in this contest was his speech to the American Irish Historical Society, in May, 1942. One strong reason for his opposition to American participation in the war had been the prospect of acts being done in the name of military exigency which might not be undone later. He saw his prediction fulfilled:

> In our efforts to protect the freedom of this country against aggression from without, we are in a situation today where we must constantly be on guard against the suppression of freedom in the United States itself. . . . We should not go one step in the modification of individual rights beyond what is actually necessary for the war effort. . . . No President has ever had as much power at the beginning of a war as has President Roosevelt, and no Congress has ever been as liberal in the granting of additional powers to the executive as has the present Congress in the last six months. Unfortunately the present administration, more than any other in the history of the country, is utterly unscrupulous in its demands for more power. . . .
>
> There is every reason to believe that many officials of the administration are using the war as an excuse for the extension in domestic affairs of a lot of unsound economic panaceas which they could not get Congress to approve in time of peace. . . . Hardly an agency is being set up which does not hope that it may continue its activities into the post-war period, including the Price Administration and the Office of Civilian Defense. . . . Last week in Washington the Attorney General of the United States told the American Society of International Law that thought must be given to the extent to which war controls must go into the post-war period, and suggested that international business corporations might be formed, with stock owned by the Government, to carry on international trade. . . .
>
> It is my firm conviction that many powers have been sought for the sake of power over domestic policy, with the war as a mere excuse. For example, the Social Security Board has been trying for some time to take over the unemployment-compensation systems of the States, together with large funds that the States have accumulated,

and do away with the merit-rating system. The moment the war broke, the President demanded from every Governor that he turn over voluntarily the State employment offices, together with many employees administering the unemployment-compensation system. The Governors unwillingly complied, although it is perfectly apparent to me that complete coordination of employment agencies could have been secured without any such arbitrary action. Already the expense of operating these employment agencies has rapidly increased. The bill to authorize the President to rearrange agencies and departments in the Government included power to transfer the functions of the Comptroller of the Treasury and the General Accounting Office, set up by the Congress to keep Executive spending within the limits of appropriation bills. This was one of the attempts made in the old reorganization bill which brought about its defeat. Only a watchful minority excepted the General Accounting Office from the terms of the bill. . . .

The War Department asked power to requisition anything and everything that it might think desirable for the war effort, including homes and personal belongings. Congress limited the power to those things needed for the Army and Navy. We have now a bill before us providing for allowances to the families of soldiers, but instead of fixing definite schedules, it proposes that the Federal Security Administration be authorized to dole out allowances to the families of soldiers at its arbitrary discretion. It can easily be seen what a tremendous political power such discretion might give over the millions of families dependent on the soldiers fighting in foreign lands.[5]

For Robert Taft, clearly, political liberty was no abstraction. American liberty was a body of chartered rights. Most of the world already had succumbed to arbitrary power; and Taft knew, with Tocqueville, that there can be such a phenomenon as "democratic despotism." His keen legal intellect foresaw a steady diminishing of the citizen's most important privileges and immunities before the claims of centralized authority, unless the public could be roused to support of the prescriptive Constitution.

In his suggested program for the Republican party in 1944, Taft called the public's attention to the fact that Americans "have had to surrender many individual rights and submit temporarily to Fascist-like regulations. The new administration will determine whether these controls are permanent or whether the multiple freedoms intended by our Constitution and Bill of Rights are restored to our people as the basis of liberty."[6] And he believed that the Roosevelt administration meant to embark upon a second New Deal, once hostilities had ended.

This was clear, he declared, from the report of the National Resources Board (abolished by Congress in spring of 1943). The report "provides for the restoration of all the New Deal agencies—the WPA, the PWA, the CCC, the NYA, and all the others—except that all of them are to be federalized on a bigger and more elaborate scale. It provides for federal aid to education and the socialization of medicine. It provides for an increased Government regulation of everyone. It recommends a Government transportation agency to control and presumably to manage the railroads, buses, air lines, and other forms of transportation. It provides for the operation by corporations in which the Government is a partner of all the power companies, aluminum companies, magnesium companies, and even shipbuilding and aircraft companies. Underlying the entire plan is the theory of unlimited Government spending. . . . It can only lead to the complete elimination of local self-government and destroy the independence of the States. It can lead only to a general socialization of industry. . . . It is the pattern for a totalitarian state."[7]

How the Eightieth Congress—and President Truman, impressed by public opinion—undid most such grand schemes, and abolished most regulations surviving from the Second World War, need not be described in detail in this book. The work of recovering civil liberty after the military emergency was Taft's, more than any other man's; for Taft was, in fact, the real leader of both Republicans and conservative Democrats in that Congress.

No serious observer has accused Taft of insincerity in his constant insistence upon the precariousness of American liberty in this age of revolution and ideology. The man clearly was incapable of dissimulation. But not seldom liberal or radical critics represented Taft's preoccupation with ordered freedom as a fixed prejudice little better than a defense of industry and commerce, the congenital attitude of a man of property; or they confounded his rigorous constitutionalism with a doctrinaire nineteenth-century liberalism. So it is worthwhile here, before examining his stand on particular questions of the day, to describe Taft's understanding of the nature of political freedom.

Liberty and Order

The American historical experience, and the American application of the rule of law, were the foundation of Taft's belief. Like most American political leaders, he rarely referred to theoretical writers on liberty; he was a man of prescription and precedent, thoroughly schooled in the law and in constitutional history.

What Richard Rovere once wrote of him is true only in part: "He believes that the underpinning of the free society is individual enterprise." It is erroneous to conclude, as did Rovere, that "to Taft, the maintenance of the free market is the first principle, and all others must scramble for position behind it."[8] Taft was no mere apologist for business and industry: for him, the rights of property owners were but part of a complex of rights.

As Taft himself said, there are limitations to liberty in a complicated society; and some limitations by government upon particular individuals actually increase the general freedom.[9] He did not relish the term "free enterprise system," because "It has seemed to me that it is too much identified with business freedom only. Liberty should have a much wider meaning."[10]

He recognized that every right is married to a duty, and that excess of liberty must end in anarchy. The immediate beneficial result of American liberty was intellectual, rather than economic: "The result of this liberty in the United States has been to permit a tremendous development of new ideas in every field of intellectual life. Those ideas have competed with each other until the best came to be accepted and led on to constantly greater development in science, in agriculture, in industry, in education, in government."[11]

No ideologue of liberty—indeed, no pure political theorist— Taft put his political faith in experience and the lessons learned by the nation and the human species. His appeal was to a constitutional structure and an economic system tested by time.

Determined though he was to restore the consciousness of true liberty in American minds, Taft knew that every freedom must have its boundaries, and must be tempered by particular circumstances. Liberty, he recognized, must be balanced against the claim of opportunity. Neither liberty nor equality of opportunity ever can be achieved to perfection: the two limit each other. This consciousness was one reason why Taft, in a number of instances, altered his position on domestic questions being debated in the Senate: over the years, circumstances had changed.

Nor did Taft dread all government; it was not a necessary evil, nor an evil at all—if confined to its proper functions. Like the Federalists, he asked repeatedly this question: For what purposes does the government act? If the preservation of liberty should require governmental action, then Taft did not shrink from that necessity. (This may be discerned in Taft's willingness to employ broad federal authority to secure civil liberties, to promote economic opportunities, and to strengthen the United States against totalist adversaries.)

As Taft expressed it, "There are many other aims besides liberty to be sought by political policy and party principle, but every policy must be justified either as an affirmative policy to secure liberty, or as a policy of human progress making no sacrifices to the god of the totalitarian state."[12] Here one must exercise what Burke called the chief virtue in a statesman—prudence. "Liberty is not license, and is not laissez-faire," he observed in one of his speeches; excessive liberty may become dangerous:

> Obviously, no man can enjoy complete liberty without entrenching upon the liberty of others. Government cannot afford to allow complete freedom, or freedom itself would disappear. Government must insure equal justice under law, or no one would be free to pursue his own life as against the reckless and selfish and unprincipled. Government must assure a reasonable equality between individuals, because if certain people enjoy all the privileges and others do not enjoy those privileges, the liberty of those others is seriously curtailed or destroyed. In many cases we must have affirmative Government action to preserve liberty. And so the preservation of liberty is not a negative program but requires a continuous legislative and executive supervision. Thus people found that if there were no Government intervention to maintain freedom of competition, some company monopolized an entire industry, and no one else was free to enter that industry or introduce a new idea. . . .

> So, also, in the field of labor-management relations, we found it necessary to have labor laws like the Wagner Act and the Norris-La Guardia Act first and the Taft-Hartley Act later. These laws were enacted so that workmen would not be at a disadvantage in dealing with a powerful employer who could deal with a thousand men at one time, and so that a small employer, or an individual union member, would not be at a disadvantage in dealing with a powerful union. In other words, these laws were passed to eliminate special privilege with power so excessive that it

destroyed the liberty of other men. The minimum wage law is based on the theory that without Government intervention oppression can occur, principally in unorganized industry. The support of farm prices is based again on the protection of a large group of small economic units against the injustices that may result from a completely free market. In the field of inflation also, Government has to step in to prevent the excessive expansion of credit which in times past has destroyed the very basis on which a free economy must rest. Certainly, a depression not only brings great hardship, but limits seriously the liberty of millions of people and the rewards to which their work entitles them. Also, as our civilization becomes more and more complex, it becomes more and more necessary to have Government regulation which will permit all to enjoy as much freedom as possible without infringing on others, as in the field of radio and television. . . .

The more complicated our life becomes, the more necessary it is to reconcile the different freedoms of different people. Our automobile traffic requires more and more red and green lights. But in all of this regulation, the main purpose behind the law must always be to maintain just as much freedom as is possible under the complicated conditions of modern life, and to prevent the constant tendency of individuals to try to achieve special privilege and special power. Our laws should be drawn by men of ability and good will in such a way as to preserve the essentials of freedom.[13]

In nothing was Robert Taft one of the "terrible simplifiers," the ideologues of one stamp or another who have plagued the world for the past two centuries. The good civil social order is not achieved through advancing one single solitary principle, to be observed to the exclusion of all others, he knew; instead, order, freedom, and justice are of equal importance to a tolerable society. He emphasized freedom much of the time because of those three objectives, freedom seemed most neglected in the age of ideology.

"The world has never had a good definition of liberty," Abraham Lincoln said once, "and the American people just now are in need of one. We all declare for liberty; but in using the same word, we do not mean the same thing."[14] Robert Taft, abhorring the vague, more than once essayed the task of describing just what he meant by "liberty." He put it thus on one occasion:

> What is liberty? It is freedom of speech and of the press, as the President said in his inaugural—but it is much more. It is the freedom of the individual to choose his own work and his life occupation, to spend his earnings as he desires to spend them, to choose the place where he desires to live, to take the job that fits him whether some union official is willing that he get it or not. It is the freedom of the local community to work out its own salvation, when it has the power to do so. It is the freedom of cities, of counties, of school districts; the freedom to educate one's children as one thinks best. It is the freedom of thought and experiment in academic institutions. It is the freedom of men in industry to run their business as they think best, so long as they do not interfere with the rights of others to do the same.[15]

Essentially, for Taft "liberty" meant the absence of coercion by others; and the duty of government was to diminish that coercion so much as possible. To Taft, freedom was the opportunity to accomplish things. "Liberty means the liberty of every individual to live his own life and think his own thoughts . . . the liberty of our families to earn their own living instead of turning it over to the government to be used in the providing of government services they may or may not want, and probably do not get."[16]

To show how Robert Taft applied such concepts of freedom to pressing public concerns, it may be helpful to examine his stand on two large issues—civil liberties, and universal military training. In either matter, his policy had little to do with personal ambition or partisan advantage.

Civil Rights and Civil Responsibilities

In recent years, it has been popular in some quarters to speak of the American Bill of Rights—and especially the First and Fifth Amendments—as if these were absolute and imprescriptible liberties, enjoying precedence over the rest of the Constitution and over all other freedoms. Robert Taft did not indulge in such distinctions, knowing that freedom of action and freedom to possess property, for instance, are at least as important as the First Amendment immunities.

Yet his concern for the civil liberties of the Bill of Rights was not less than that he felt for other freedoms. To contend against subversive theories and the suppression of truth through governmental propaganda, Taft said once, Congress must be vigilant in the defense "of freedom of speech and other press, for upon the preservation of that right depends nearly every other individual right declared in the Bill of Rights."[17]

No member of the Senate was more intelligently opposed to Communism than was Taft; he strongly supported, for instance, legislation meant to bring "the Communist Party out into the open so the people can see who they are."[18] Proposals to declare membership in the party unlawful, however, he believed to be "not possible, constitutional, or advisable."[19] At Milwaukee, in 1948, Taft stated that "As a matter of policy, it is somewhat doubtful whether we gain much by outlawing Communism and driving it underground. . . . Under our Constitution, we cannot, and should not, make it illegal for an American citizen to think Communism or express his opinions, so long as he does not advocate a violent overthrow of the government."[20] Somewhat similarly, he opposed governmental intervention in the affairs of state universities and colleges, even where the influence of Communists was in question; academic freedom and its limitations should be left to the regular administrators, trustees, and faculties of educational institutions.

Senator Taft's views concerning the civil rights of Negro citizens and their exercise of the franchise are of especial interest today. Here was a field in which Taft's own principles sometimes were in tension, so that he found it necessary to balance one body of rights against another. He strongly affirmed the political equality of all citizens, without reference to color; also he believed in maintaining the powers of state and local governments, against the encroachments of central authority.

Taft's attempt to reconcile these two genuine claims of right sometimes brought him into collision with other Republicans. In 1936, during his campaign against Taft for delegates to the Republican National Convention, for instance, Senator Borah accused Taft of caring nothing for "constitutional integrity or states' rights" because of Taft's support for an anti-lynching bill before Congress.[21]

Taft's most lively role in this prolonged debate over the rights of colored citizens came in 1947, when he led the fight to prevent Senator Theodore Bilbo, a Democrat from Mississippi, from taking his seat in the Senate at the opening session of the Republican-dominated Eightieth Congress. Bilbo had been charged with violating the Hatch Act through improper campaign expenditures, and with intimidating Negro voters through violently anti-Negro speeches during his campaign. The latter charge, if proven, would bar Bilbo from taking the oath of office, on the ground that he had not been lawfully elected—although Taft pointed out that the Senate need not specify any particular reason for excluding a prospective member.[22] The debate which ensued followed partisan lines, every Republican supporting Taft, and most Democrats standing back of Bilbo. After much acrimonious parliamentary maneuvering, the question was settled by the withdrawal of Bilbo, who was suffering from cancer.

In general, Taft got along well with conservative Democratic senators from the South; but Senator Bilbo's anti-Negro ferocity, and his demagoguery, Taft could not abide in the Senate.

There existed constitutional and prudential limits, nevertheless, beyond which Taft declined to pass in the attempt to secure equality of civil rights for Negroes. In 1945 he voted against a compulsory federal Fair Employment Practices Committee, declaring that "Race prejudice is a deplorable thing . . . but I don't believe it is possible to legislate human prejudices out of existence."[23] As he explained in 1952, "I have supported a federal Fair Employment Practices Committee on a voluntary basis to study the whole problem of discrimination in industrial employment. This seems to me primarily the duty of the States, but I do think the Federal Government has a responsibility and can at least set up a commission to study the problem, present the facts, and bring about the removal of discrimination by education and persuasion." He defended his vote of 1945, adding, "I have been opposed to writing a Federal law giving every man who is refused employment the right to sue the possible employer on the ground that he was influenced by some discriminatory motive or prejudice. This seems to me an interference by Federal Government in millions of employer-employee relationships—the regulation of business and individual life. It is just that kind of regulation and interference in other fields which I have always strenuously opposed. I particularly object to giving some Federal board power to pass on the motives of the employer, a fact almost impossible to determine in many cases. . . . In general, this is one of those fields where constant improvement can be brought about by education, whereas an attempt to force the same improvement would create bitter resentment."[24]

When the question of racial desegregation in public schools arose, Taft found it necessary to balance against his strict construction of the Constitution, and against his belief in states' powers, his concern for Negroes' civil equality. Beginning in 1938, the Supreme Court made its gradual way toward the abolition of school segregation, culminating in the Brown decision of 1954. In a series of cases involving segregation in the graduate schools of state universities, the Court—though it evaded the "separate but equal" doctrine of *Plessy v. Ferguson* which later was repudiated in the Brown case—interpreted the "equal" aspect of the formula so rigorously as to make compliance almost impossible under racial segregation. In two significant cases of 1950, the Court held that states barring the entrance of Negroes to the graduate schools of state universities were in violation of the guarantees of equal protection of the laws, under the Fourteenth Amendment—in one of these decisions, the separate state-university graduate school for Negroes being held inferior to the graduate school for whites.

Taft did not dissent from these decisions. In 1952 he said, "I approve of the general position taken by the Supreme Court requiring states to furnish equal educational facilities to their citizens of all classes."[25] This had been his stand a year earlier, in an address to the colored students of North Carolina College. Taft then had told his audience that he "entirely approved" the Supreme Court's decisions opening Southern universities to Negroes; and he added, "I would vote to abolish them [segregated colleges] in the District of Columbia or any other place where the Federal Government has jurisdiction." But he appended to this declaration an important qualification: "The control of education under our Constitution is in the jurisdiction of the states and not of the Federal Government. As long as states provide equal educational facilities for white and colored children in the primary schools, I do not think the Federal Government has the constitutional power to require a state to change its established system of education."[26]

This qualification was not calculated to please the audience. Taft's position was that if qualitative equality of segregated schools existed in fact, then the federal government possessed no constitutional authority to intervene; presumably he would not have assented to Chief Justice Warren's later decision that "separate educational facilities are *inherently* unequal."

Negroes interested in politics generally were friendly toward Senator Taft. One colored citizen of Ohio remarked,

"Our Senator Taft's record is wonderful, but I am not sure that all of our people understand his motives. Senator Taft is not pro-Negro. He is not pro-white. He is not pro-labor, nor pro-management. The man has some strange passion for justice. He would work just as hard to stop us tomorrow if he believed that we were oppressing anybody. And he will tell you so if you ask him. That gives what he does more weight with me. He is not trying to win our votes so much as he is trying to do what is right."[27]

In a *Collier's* magazine interview, near the end of his life, Senator Taft remarked, "I have supported the anti-lynch legislation because I feel that the Federal Government has the right to protect a man against the action or failure to act of local governments in matters affecting his life and liberty. I have supported all bills to eliminate discrimination in the armed services. The Federal Government has an interest in seeing that interstate commerce is also conducted without discrimination. Wherever the Federal Government has a responsibility, I think it should be exercised."

Asked to explain his general position on civil rights, Taft replied that civil liberties could be understood only in the context of the Constitution; therefore an unqualified endorsement of Negro claims, in the abstract, was impossible for him. "Broadly speaking," he continued, "the question is whether I feel that the Federal Government should intervene to protect individuals in their constitutional rights against the action of other individuals and state and local governments." He believed that the federal authorities should intervene when such action clearly was sanctioned by the Constitution. Sometimes, nevertheless, he ventured beyond indubitable constitutionality in this field: the constitutionality of bills to repeal by federal legislation the state poll taxes was in dispute at the time Taft spoke, but he supported such legislation "because I think that the federal government does have an interest in seeing that every man has the right to vote in federal elections."[28]

In the whole debate over Negroes' rights which extended from the end of the Second World War until his death,

Robert Taft's was one of the more sensible voices, pleading for prudential reform not inconsonant with American political principle.

Universal Military Training

Taft's defenses of individual freedom are too numerous for a full discussion here; his best-known successful intervention against a proposed arbitrary bill, President Truman's plan for conscripting striking railwaymen, will be touched upon in a later chapter. For sustained effort, however, his struggle against compulsory universal military training, beginning near the close of the Second World War, is foremost in Taft's civil-freedom record.

Even as demobilization of the enormous army of the Second World War commenced, powerful voices were raised in New York, Washington, and elsewhere to demand that all young men should be required to serve a term in the armed forces during time of peace. In part, this plan was based on the theory that the nation must be ready for some other military emergency; in part, it reflected the ideas of William James's essay "The Moral Equivalent of War," and other proposals for direction of American youth. And it reflected, in not a few instances, a taste for mass regulation for the sake of mass regulation.

No one in Congress exceeded Senator Taft in determination to resist Soviet aggression; but to him universal military training was the "armed horde," the *levée en masse* of the Jacobins, dangerous to constitutional government and an invasion of personal freedom. Also he believed the plan to be militarily obsolete and unnecessary. His first important speech against the scheme came in his address at Gettysburg National Cemetery, May 30, 1945; he was to repeat this argument on many later occasions.

"It is useless to destroy totalitarianism in Germany and Japan," he said, "and then establish it in the United States.

. . . Government controls such as peacetime military conscription, which would have been indignantly rejected in the nineteenth century, are given serious consideration, even in this country. . . . Many people who would indignantly deny any soft feeling for state control are advocates of measures which lead inevitably in that direction because they are dissatisfied with the necessarily slow progress involved in a government where all the people are given a voice. . . . The war has required a suspension of many freedoms, and the people have become so used to regulations that they almost forget what freedom is. The danger of totalitarian government is that the people do get used to it, as to a narcotic."[29]

The power to subject young men to complete discipline was "the most serious limitation on freedom that can be imagined," he concluded. Taft was no pacifist, and did not object to military conscription in time of war. But to go beyond real military necessity was another matter. He had taken part in defeating the Austin-Wadsworth "work or fight" bill of 1943, and earlier had opposed the Selective Service Act of 1940—before the nation had declared war. He proposed to rely upon a professional army, expert in the use of modern weapons, possibly supplemented by a volunteer reserve, intensively trained during summers and other periods.

After the Communist *coup d'état* in Czechoslovakia (February 1948), and General Lucius Clay's secret warning to the Truman administration that Soviet Russia might take yet more aggressive action in Europe, President Truman proposed to Congress on March 17, 1948, that the United States embark upon a permanent program of universal military training, as distinguished from the "draft," or selective service. Truman told Congress, "Universal training is the only feasible means by which the civilian components of our armed forces can be built up to the strength required if we are to be prepared for emergencies. Our ability to mobilize large numbers of trained men in time of emergency could forestall future conflict and, together with other measures of national policy, could restore stability to the world."[30]

The Truman proposal was made while Taft dominated the Eightieth Congress and after he had been speaking for several years against universal training. He declared that he would fight Truman's UMT to the bitter end. In a speech at Fremont, Nebraska, on April 7, 1948, he suggested that the constitutional principle of civilian control of the military was in question:

"We are met at the outset by the suggestion that we civilians can know nothing of the problem, that every decision must be made by miltiary authorities who are experts on these problems. Of course this argument cannot be true. The ultimate decision on over-all questions of defense and even of military policy must be made by a civilian government. If we admit the final authority of the military to decide these problems, it means that they will soon have in their hands the entire economic and political future of the United States. No student of government can be found who advocates the leaving of final decisions in time of peace, or even perhaps in time of war, to a military commander."

Should volunteering be insufficient, a draft might be necessary—but not universal military training. "In this whole field there is no reason why our approach should not be governed by the same principles of liberty as must guide other Government programs. UMT is a return to the New Deal belief that results can only be accomplished by Government compulsion, and power given to Government bureaus. The New Dealers have scoffed at the idea that the people can work out their own salvation, or work out their own problems, without Government direction. . . . These methods have failed in the field of economic control. They have failed even to provide the education and social security which is the greatest promise of the New Deal. . . . I believe that in providing a defense against possible foreign attacks on the liberty of our people, we cannot adopt methods by which we ourselves destroy our own liberty."[31]

Despite the strong pressures behind President Truman's UMT plan, Congress listened to Senator Taft and rejected universal military training. There was enacted instead the Selective Service Act of 1948, requiring all men between the ages of eighteen and twenty-five to register, and making liable for twenty-one months of service those between nineteen and twenty-five. Eighteen-year-old volunteers, to the number of 161,000, might enlist for one year, and by joining the reserves for six years would be exempt from the draft provisions—in accord with Taft's early recommendations for a volunteer reserve. Taft voted for this bill. From 1948 to 1966, neither universal military training nor an all-inclusive "national service" was seriously proposed by a national administration.

Although until late in life he possessed only limited knowledge of military matters—and occasionally had been naïve, before the Second World War, on such subjects—Taft had demolished, in the eyes of Congress and the public, the uneasy case for universal military training.* It was not a good means for raising competent troops, he had argued in 1945; nor would it produce incidental benefits:

> It is said that it will teach the boys discipline and that they need it. My own opinion is that we need more initiative and original thinking and less discipline, rather than more. Our present Army is not the most disciplined in the world, but there isn't any better army, for the simple reason that the boys do some thinking for themselves. It is said that the Army will improve their health, and that they need it because so many failed to pass the strict health-requirements of the Army. As a matter of fact, the great bulk of defects were those relating to teeth, eyes, mental, nervous, and heart conditions, all of which had arisen before the age of conscription. . . . The argument that it would improve the morals of our boys has almost been dropped because of its foolishness. If there is one place where morals will not be improved, it is in the vicinity of army camps. It is true that there are some boys who are benefited by army control, but to improve a few, let us not change the whole character of the American life

* During the First World War, Taft twice volunteered for military service, but was rejected because of his imperfect eyesight.

which, I believe, has been the cause of success in this war. It is said that we are going to teach the boys citizenship in the camps. This argument makes clear a real danger in the whole system. By handing boys over for twelve months to the arbitrary and complete domination of the Government, we put it in the power of the Government to indoctrinate them with the political doctrines then popular with the Government. It has all the dangers of Federal education and none of its advantages.[32]

In this successful struggle for freedom from military regimentation, Taft beat down the advocacy of some of the more important newspapers and publicists in the country, of the Army itself, of the Secretary of State (General Marshall), the Secretary of War, and the "Citizens' Emergency Committee for Universal Military Training," headed by Owen J. Roberts, formerly a Justice of the Supreme Court. No senator since Taft's time has exerted a comparable power to restrain the proposals of the executive branch and the armed services.

The Moral Basis of Freedom

Despite the scowling menace of an "armed doctrine," Communism, supported by Russian and Chinese force of arms; despite all the wars and rumors of war since the defeat of Germany and Japan; despite the triumph of the total state in much of the world—the United States of America has preserved a free society, ever since the end of the Second World War. The growth of central political activity in America has been confined principally to the fields of social welfare, education, and civil rights—areas in which Taft had no objection on principle to some federal action, though it should be undertaken after thorough discussion and tempered by prudence. Various measures, notably the Medicare Act, have gone much beyond what Robert Taft would have approved; still, "Fair Deal," "New Frontier," and "Great Society" programs have not diminished liberty so substantially as Robert Taft feared that the theories of the New Deal might do, should they be given a second lease of life.

In this setting of bounds to the sphere of centralized political power, Taft had a considerable part, even though it cannot be measured accurately. Arbitrary power increases in proportion as public and private morality decline, he said more than once. The example of his own integrity may have done as much to preserve freedom founded upon a moral order as did his labor in the Senate.

"The moral vacuum in government has extended to the leaders in many private fields," he wrote in 1950. "We have developed a system of pressure-groups—men in various fields who have banded themselves together to protect the interests of their groups. The net effect of pressure-group activity, though much of it is beneficial, is to reduce political principle as a force in the determination of government policy. . . . Perhaps the people have lost their sense of moral integrity because their leaders have lost it, but I don't believe so. I think it is a feeling of hopeless disgust rather than one of approval. Washington is a long way off, and most people have a sense of helplessness in trying to change what seems to have become government's accepted practices. . . . Certainly the time has come for a moral revival which will restore to our people a confidence in the integrity of government and in the principles of their leaders. They will have to be aroused to the fact that their votes can make a real change in the quality of government. It is of critical importance to restore in our government the principle set forth more than one hundred years ago by Henry Clay: 'Government is a trust, and the officers of government are trustees; and both the trust and the trustees are created for the benefit of the people.' "[33]

An able teacher imparts as much by what he *is* as by what he says. Similarly, Robert Taft accomplished as much for American liberty under law by his example as an eminent politician governed by moral principle, as he did by his congressional opposition to the impersonal and despotic tendencies of modern society.

Notes, CHAPTER IV

1. Robert A. Taft, "Freedom, the Key to Progress," speech before the National Canners' Association, Chicago, February 21, 1953; printed in the *Congressional Record*, 83rd Congress, 1st Session, Vol. 99, Part 9 (February 25, 1953), p. A876.

2. Robert A. Taft, "A 1944 Program for the Republicans," *Saturday Evening Post*, Vol. 216, No. 24 (December 11, 1943), p. 17.

3. Robert A. Taft, "An Order after the War," speech before the Ohio State Bar Association at Toledo, October 24, 1941; printed in the *Congressional Record*, 77th Congress, 1st Session, Vol. 87, Part 14 (October 27, 1941), p. A4838.

4. *Ibid.*, p. A4837.

5. Robert A. Taft, "Unity and Freedom of the Press," speech before the American Irish Historical Society, New York, May 2, 1942; printed in the *Congressional Record*, 77th Congress, 2nd Session, Vol. 88, Part 9 (May 4, 1942), pp. A1622–A1623.

6. Taft, "A 1944 Program," *op. cit.*, p. 17.

7. *Ibid.*, p. 50.

8. Richard Rovere, "Taft: Is This the Best We've Got?" *Harper's*, Vol. 196, No. 1175 (April 1948), p. 295.

9. See Duncan Norton-Taylor, "Robert Taft's Congress," *Fortune*, Vol. XLVII, No. 2 (August 1953), p. 142.

10. Taft, "Freedom, the Key to Progress," *op. cit.*, p. A877.

11. *Ibid.*

12. Robert A. Taft, "The Republican Party," *Fortune*, Vol. XXXIX, No. 4 (April 1949), p. 109.

13. Taft, "Freedom, the Key to Progress," *op. cit.*, pp. A877–A878.

14. Abraham Lincoln, address at Sanitary Fair, Baltimore Maryland, April 18, 1864; printed in *Collected Works of Abraham Lincoln* (edited by Roy Basler), Vol. VII, p. 301.

15. Taft, "The Republican Party," *op. cit.*, p. 109.
16. Taft, "Freedom, the Key to Progress," *op. cit.*, p. A877.
17. Taft, "Unity and Freedom of the Press," *op. cit.*, p. A1623.
18. Reported in *The New York Times*, February 18, 1947, p. 28.
19. *Ibid.*, June 5, 1948, p. 2.
20. *Ibid.*, May 9, 1948, p. 46.
21. *Ibid.*, May 14, 1936, p. 6.
22. *Ibid.*, January 2, 1947, p. 1.
23. See Duncan Norton-Taylor, "Robert Taft's Congress," *op. cit.*, p. 145.
24. Robert A. Taft, "What I Believe," *Collier's*, Vol. 129, No. 15 (April 12, 1952), p. 83.
25. *Ibid.*, p. 84.
26. Speech at North Carolina College, quoted in the *New York Times*, December 19, 1951, p. 5.
27. Quoted by Zora Neale Hurston, "A Negro Voter Sizes up Taft," *Saturday Evening Post*, Vol. 224, No. 23 (December 8, 1951), p. 150.
28. Taft, "What I Believe," *op. cit.*, p. 84.
29. Robert A. Taft, "Compulsory Military Training in Peacetime Will Destroy Government by the People," speech delivered at Gettysburg National Cemetery, May 30, 1945; printed in the *Congressional Record*, 79th Congress, 1st Session, 1945, Vol. 91, Part 11 (May 31, 1945), p. A2609.
30. See *The Truman Administration: a Documentary History*, edited by Barton J. Bernstein and Allen J. Matusow (New York, 1966), pp. 269–271.
31. Robert A. Taft, "Universal Military Training and National Defense," speech delivered at Fremont, Nebraska, April 7, 1948; printed in the *Congressional Record*, 80th Congress, 2nd Session, Vol. 94, Part 10 (April 20, 1948), pp. A2359–A2360.
32. Robert A. Taft, "Compulsory Military Training in Peacetime," *op. cit.*, p. A2610.
33. Robert A. Taft, "The Dangerous Decline of Political Morality," *Reader's Digest*, Vol. 57, No. 343 (November 1950), p. 156.

CHAPTER V

The Restraint of Power

The Primacy of Justice

"As the apostle of strict constitutionalism, as the chief
defense attorney for the conservative way of life and government, Robert Alphonso Taft was undeterred by the possibilities of injury to his party's precarious position or his own
Presidential prospects. To him, justice was at stake, and all
other concerns were trivial."[1]

So John F. Kennedy wrote, in his *Profiles in Courage*, of
Senator Taft's denunciation of the Nuremberg Trials. To
maintain the rule of law in a time of violence and opportunism
was Taft's sternest endeavor, from beginning to end of his
public life. Virgil says that the good man is a law-abiding
traditionalist; and Taft's enunciation of the principles of justice, no matter what the mood of the crowd, reminds one of a
passage in Cicero's *Republic:*

"Long before our own time, the customs of our ancestors
molded admirable men, and in turn these eminent men upheld
the ways and institutions of our forebears. Our age, nevertheless, inherited the Republic as if it were some beautiful paint-
ing of bygone days, its colors already fading through great
age; and not only has our time neglected to freshen the colors
of the picture, but we have failed to preserve its form and
outline. For what remains to us, nowadays, of the ancient

85

customs on which the commonwealth, we are told, was founded? We see them so lost in oblivion that they are not merely neglected, but quite forgot. And what am I to say of the men? For our customs have perished for want of men to stand by them, and now we are called to an account, so that we stand impeached like men accused of capital crimes, compelled to plead our own cause. Through our vices, rather than from happenstance, we retain the word *republic* long after we have lost the reality."

If Taft, upholding the venerable principles of law, did not quite consider his time a sunken age, still he believed that America, with the rest of the world, was sliding toward a gulf of injustice; and mighty exertions would be required to secure freedom, order, and justice for unborn generations. A government that had been one of laws, and not of men, now squinted toward arbitrary power. Effectively to restrain that power—which, once made absolute, would corrupt absolutely—was Taft's essential labor. In this chapter, we take up two aspects of Taft's endeavor to maintain a constitutional order and to do justice to all men: his championship of Congress against the Executive, and his remarks on the Nuremberg Trials. The first of these ran through all his career, over fourteen years; the second was only an incident, but a significant and characteristic instance of Taft's rectitude and fortitude.

That centralized and consolidated power was nominally "democratic" did not make it harmless, Taft understood. In the radio debates between Taft and T. V. Smith, Representative Smith had said, "The greatest success of the Constitution . . . is that in a century and a half it has won the people from an ancient distrust of government to an acceptance of it as their friend. And why not, pray? A democratic government *is* the people themselves incorporated to make corporate competitors useful . . ."

Taft had replied, in effect, as Thomas Jefferson would have replied: in matters of power, we dare not put our trust in man, but must bind him down with the chains of the Constitution. Government may restrain "the power of wealth"; but "it must be certain that it does not substitute for this threat from the power of wealth the threat from the power of arbitrary government itself."[2] Only regular obedience to the rule of law could save even a democratic society from the tyranny of a temporary majority or of a plebiscitary master.

Until a little while before Taft entered the Senate, the principal check upon the abuse of executive or legislative power, in the American constitutional structure, had been the Supreme Court of the United States. Robert Taft conceded that the Court had not always been inerrable: probably "in their zeal to protect these rights [of the Bill of Rights] the courts have given too much effect to the so-called due-process clause," for instance. "Whether we wish to abandon any of those rights may be debatable, but we can hardly criticize the courts for giving them effect."[3]

Yet that judicial bulwark against arbitrary measures had given way in 1937. Although Congress had rejected Roosevelt's plan for packing the Supreme Court with new justices of his mode of thinking, in effect Roosevelt had his way. Intimidated, the Court accepted the New Deal, and as justices retired, Roosevelt was enabled to appoint men of his choosing. The foundation of this "constitutional revolution" in 1937 had been laid earlier by legal scholars, historians, and professors of politics—J. Allen Smith, Charles A. Beard, Edward S. Corwin, and others. The Supreme Court's declaration, in 1935, that the National Recovery Act was unconstitutional amounted to almost the last stand of the judicial branch against the executive. The Roosevelt Court would interpose no real obstacles to the expansion of federal authority over the states, or to the most elaborately liberal interpretations of constitutional restraints upon political power.

As Taft was to emphasize in his debates with Smith, the framers of the Constitution had "imposed three great limitations on the power of the national government": federalism, separation of powers, and the Bill of Rights. "The Founders knew that preservation of local home rule was essential to real liberty. . . ." They had "carefully separated the powers of the national government between the executive, legislature, and judiciary, so that no one branch should be able to exercise all of even the limited powers given to the Federal Government. . . ." And the Bill of Rights "provides, in effect, that even the power of the majority of the people shall never be used to tyrannize over any minority."[4]

These dikes restricting power gave way in 1937. A part, at least, of the American public was alarmed at Roosevelt's high-handed way with the Supreme Court; and, as Taft remarked, the Republican gains in the election of 1938 were a consequence. But Roosevelt's impaired control of Congress, and his partial loss of popularity, did not restore the Court as effective guardian of the demarcation between state and central powers, between executive and national legislature, or between political authority and the citizen.

So Robert Taft, once in the Senate, addressed himself to an endeavor to accomplish, through the legislative branch, that hedging and curbing of power which the Supreme Court no longer attempted. If the Court would not uphold the Constitution, still the Congress might. Having set his hand to that plow, with some success he worked until 1953 to restore the old balance between the legislative and executive branches of the federal government.

On the eve of the "constitutional revolution," Taft had commenced his counterassault. In his article "Sidestepping the Constitution," published in *The Review of Reviews* in the autumn of 1936, this Ohio lawyer had cudgelled Corwin and other advocates of the radical expansion of Congress's powers over interstate commerce.

"The revival of bitter criticism both of the Constitution and of the Supreme Court," Taft wrote then, "is due to one thing only. The basis of New Deal policy is a planned economy. It desires to substitute for the competitive business system under which this country has been built up a system in which government directs all business and financial activity. . . . Experience has shown that once goverment undertakes to regulate wages and prices, it must go on, if its regulation is to be effective, to control all the minor practices in the business which have an effect on price, which means every detail of the business. This can only be done by complete control of all production."

No such power was to be found in the Constitution, Taft declared. "All of the sophistry of the Constitutional innovators was swept away by the decisions of the Supreme Court in the NRA, AAA, and Guffey Coal decisions. These were not in any sense political decisions opposed to the New Deal. The NRA decision was unanimous. They rather reaffirmed the fundamental principles of American government. They held that the national government was one of limited powers, which did not include control of manufacturing and agriculture. They held that the commerce clause and the spending power could not be used as subterfuges to give the national government power it was not intended to have."

But the New Dealers were resolved not to submit to the Court's decisions. They would interfere, in one fashion or another, with the Supreme Court. "The President and his supporters are prepared to advocate a direct amendment changing the whole basis of the Constitution, if that should be necessary, but the reaction to the President's statement showed them that direct amendment would not be a popular issue. They are determined, if possible, to effect a constitutional change by the President's power to appoint a majority of the Supreme Court, if he is reelected."

This would make the Constitution little better than a scrap of parchment, Taft concluded: "If men are appointed to the Court for the very purpose of abdicating its functions, of thinning out the fundamental principles of the Constitution, of destroying the federal form of government and the division of powers, then the whole basis of the American Constitution is at an end. There will remain nothing to prevent an all-powerful state determining the activities and existence of its citizens. There will remain nothing to prevent dictatorship as we see in many countries abroad. . . . The plans of President Roosevelt and his New Deal supporters to swamp the Court with judges who believe that constitutional principles are weak as water will mean the twilight not only of the Supreme Court, but ultimately of American liberty and American democracy."[5]

The transformation of the Court predicted by Taft came abruptly, even before the defeat of Roosevelt's Court-packing design. Justice Roberts changed sides, and began to endorse the constitutionality of New Deal legislation; the floodgates were opened. On March 29, 1937, the Supreme Court upheld the constitutionality of the minimum-wage act of the state of Washington, reversing a decision in a similar case ten months earlier. On April 12, the National Labor Relations Act was declared constitutional; so, six weeks thereafter, was the Social Security Act. With the retirement of Justices Sutherland and Van Devanter, a Rooseveltian majority on the Court became invincible; and between 1938 and 1944, Roosevelt was to appoint nine new Justices.

Yet the victory of the New Deal was a narrow one, and Roosevelt had little time in which to act. Although the Supreme Court was his, the Congress had begun to move in an opposite direction.

Taft against the Executive Force

By the time Robert Taft took his seat in the Senate, the endeavor to restrain power through the Supreme Court had been lost. The energetic new senator, therefore, directed himself to the Congress and the public. All three branches of government, he believed, had spread beyond their constitutional limitations. While Congress was diminishing the powers of states on the one hand, it was delegating its own powers to the President on the other. President and Supreme Court assumed whatever powers they could extract from Congress.

The national legislature might redress this balance. Congress's power over the purse is unlimited, and so it can check the Executive; as for the Supreme Court, Congress controls its appellate jurisdiction—and, if necessary, can propose constitutional amendments. But could Congress be induced to look jealously upon the aggrandizement of Executive and Court—and, at least as important, upon its own powers? With few exceptions, until Taft took his seat, Congress had given President Roosevelt whatever authority he desired.

In his debates with Smith, Taft observed, "It is hard to concentrate responsibility in a group of 531 men, but I feel confident it can be done."[6] If he did not succeed altogether, in the years that followed, nevertheless he did much to make the Congress such a responsible power—and a power, sometimes, for self-restraint, as well as restriction upon the Executive—as the framers of the Constitution had meant Congress to be.[7]

It was during the Second World War, when Congress delegated tremendous authority to the President, that Senator Taft protested most strongly. As Dr. Roland Young concludes, "During the War, there was a propensity to delegate to the President in somewhat sweeping terms . . . broad, almost boundless grants of authority, which allowed the President to mobilize the resources of the country and to reorganize, and perhaps create, government agencies."[8]

The dangers accompanying such delegation of legislative authority, apparent during Roosevelt's first administration, were described by Taft in a speech to the Ohio Bar Association a few months before America's declaration of war against the Axis powers. "The Founders of the Constitution knew that nearly every democracy in the history of the world had finally degenerated into a tyranny, an empire, or a kingdom. They knew that had happened because gradually all the powers of the government were delegated by the people to one man or a small group of men. Delegated usually in an emergency, they were never surrendered. For that reason they set up a written constitution to be interpreted by independent courts. They retained vast powers in the hands of the states, and delegated only national powers to the federal government. Even these limited powers were divided between the Executive, Congress, and the courts, and the courts were given the job of protecting individual freedom against the powers of government."[9]

In August 1942, Taft delivered a radio address in Cleveland, defending Congress against attacks by the liberals, who were angered at congressional resistance to Roosevelt's proposals ever since 1938. Taft was conducting his campaign on two fronts. Simultaneously, he reproached his congressional colleagues for abdicating their responsibilities, and warded off the assaults of the liberals who demanded greater subservience to the Executive force. "The criticism of Congress seems to have been inspired at the present moment by those who wish to destroy Congress as an institution," he stated. Should this body of critics succeed, "Congress would be as subservient to the Executive as it is in Russia or in Germany. It is vitally important that we have congressmen who will stand up against many of the Administration's proposals, supposed to relate to the War, but actually having more effect on domestic affairs."[10]

Many of these criticisms were without foundation, Taft continued: Congress should not be blamed for the unpreparedness of the Army and the Navy, because "for the last ten years Congress has appropriated every cent recommended by the President and by the heads of the Army and the Navy"; this was true, too, of the fortification of Guam, and the construction of synthetic-rubber factories.

Congress could not conduct the war, Taft pointed out in his speeches during this period, but Congress had the duty of investigating the conduct of operations. "Criticism should be both temperate and constructive, and in the field of current military and naval operations it can hardly rise to a higher level than that of suggestion. . . . But the most important function of Congress relating to the Army arises when the interests of the Army conflict with those of other essential war purposes."[11]

The Overman Act, giving the President authority to reorganize the government, had produced much confusion which Congress should correct. And the doctrinaire theorists of the vast federal bureaucracy should be chastened by Congressional scrutiny. "There is no doubt in my mind that many members of the Administration have deliberately sought power much greater than required for the war for the purpose of extending the regulation of business and individuals with a view to the continuation of such regulation after the war. Every law that has been written has requested wide-open power. . . . Congress must have the independence when the end of the war has in fact occurred to declare the termination of these powers. For there is a real danger after the war that an attempt will be made to extend these powers indefinitely. . . . Undoubtedly many liberties must be suspended during the war, but Congress should be alert to see that no liberty is suspended unless is it absolutely necessary for success in the war."[12]

In October, Taft praised the War Resources Administration, established by Congress to oversee the production of munitions, and the investigating committee headed by Senator Truman. Yet he thought that Congress should be less subservient to the Executive. "The administrative agencies, like the draft boards, must pass on the individual capacity of each man, but they should do so under clear rules laid down by law according to principles established by Congress. Any attempt by the Executive to seize such power breaks down the very democratic system for which we are fighting throughout all the continents of the world to preserve. That system depends on the making of the people's laws by the people's representatives."[13]

Taft was making headway. In the summer of 1943, he told the Alabama Bar Association that "the most encouraging thing about this Congress" was its "assertion of independence. . . . Whenever possible, it is recalling the powers delegated to the President by subservient Congresses."[14]

During 1943, Congress abolished several New Deal agencies, notably the Works Progress Administration, the Civilian Conservation Corps, the National Youth Administration, and the National Resources Planning Board. Taft was particularly pleased that Congress diminished the functions of Elmer Davis's Office of War Information. Because Congressmen believed that propaganda sent abroad might assist the armed forces, it did not abolish the foreign branch of this office, though Taft thought it was "full of crackpots and incompetents and communists." But the domestic branch of the office was eliminated. "If we are going to maintain free speech in this country," he commented, "we do not need Federal propaganda. . . . For ten years we have been guided by the New Deal philosophy. It has opened up many lines of progress. . . . But it has recklessly disregarded the most fundamental principles established in the American Constitution. . . . This Congress has been determined that these principles be re-established and that further progress be within the framework of the principles of American democracy."[15]

With every year that Taft spent in the Senate, checks upon Executive power increased—in considerable part because of his astute management of the opposition. But he did not relax his vigilance. "I believe that freedom can only be preserved if we retain government by the people all the time. I heard a United States Senator argue that we could have freedom and democracy even though Congress delegated all its powers to the President during the war and adjourned, because, he said, we could meet again and take those powers away. There are two fallacies in that view. While that form of government lasts, there is no freedom and it is not government by the people. Secondly, if it lasts too long, the powers granted by the people are never returned to them. That has been the history of popular government from the days of Greece and Rome through the Middle Ages to Germany and Japan today."[16]

A good example of Taft's struggle to prevent the Executive force from usurping Congress' authority was his concern with war-time control of prices. With the increase of military expenditure, prices rose rapidly; on July 30, 1941, Roosevelt asked Congress to impose ceilings on prices. The attack on Pearl Harbor induced Congress to comply: in January 1942,

Congress authorized a new Office of Price Administration. But prices continued to rise: by March 1942, the price of food had increased 4.9 per cent since Pearl Harbor, and the price of clothing 7.7 per cent. Congress took no action. The President informed Congress on September 7 that if Congress should fail to lower price ceilings on farm commodities within three weeks, then he would dissolve by decree the existing farm-parity law.

Roosevelt's message contained these ominous words: "I ask the Congress to take this action by the 1st of October. Inaction on your part by that date will leave me with an inescapable responsibility to the people of this country to see to it that the war effort is no longer imperilled by the threat of economic chaos. In the event that the Congress shall fail to act and act adequately, I shall accept the responsibility and I will act. At the same time that farm prices are stabilized, wages can and will be stabilized. This I will do."[17]

As Roland Young comments, this threat by the President "appears to have been a rash and unnecessary challenge to constitutional procedures. Congress came within a day of meeting the President's imposed deadline, and this quick response, humiliating as it was under such goading, prevented the development of a constitutional crisis. However, the threat was not forgotten, and the episode created suspicion and distrust which continued to harass the administration for the remainder of the war."[18]

Indignant but not surprised, Senator Taft condemned Roosevelt's arrogant language and action—and was much abused by the liberal part of the press for his obduracy. The new legislation passed by Congress at Roosevelt's prodding became the Stabilization Act of 1942. But from that time forward, Congress looked with hostility upon fresh presidential demands for more power, and rejected several such bills sponsored by the Roosevelt administration. Meanwhile, despite the Stabilization Act, prices continued to rise; within six months after its enactment, the cost of living was six per cent higher. Executive orders, and a system of consumer subsidies determined by the Executive, were Roosevelt's response. Though the subsidies, paid through the Commodity Credit Corporation, were unpopular with Congress as an invasion of the legislative prerogative, Roosevelt's use of his veto extended the life of the CCC until June 30, 1945.

In the end, it was Senator Taft who contrived that Congress should regain its control over subsidies and price controls. When price legislation expired in June 1944, Taft's accomplished parliamentary tactics combined the renewal of price controls with the subsidy program in a single bill. The subsidies were made more equitable, and the bill provided that in the future Congress—not the Executive—would appropriate funds for the subsidies. To avoid renewed controversy over subsidies and to ensure price controls, the Roosevelt administration was compelled to accept Taft's provisions joining price controls with subsidies, and restoring authority in the whole field to the Congress. In a predominantly Democratic Congress, Taft had checked Roosevelt severely.

The Contest with President Truman

From necessity, and from his own experience in the Senate, President Truman was gentler with Congress than his predecessor had been; yet his conception of the presidential office differed little from Roosevelt's. Taft's response to encroachment by the Truman Executive Force upon Constitution and Congress was swift and effectual, most notably when President Truman proposed to draft striking railwaymen into the armed forces. The controversy over Truman's seizure of the steel mills, near the end of Taft's career in opposition, sufficiently illustrates Senator Taft's resourcefulness during the Truman years.

At the climax of a long dispute between the managers of the steel industry and the United Steel Workers, the federal mediation service and the federal wage-stabilization board had failed to obtain a settlement. To prevent a steel strike, on April

8, 1952, Truman directed the Secretary of Commerce to seize and operate nearly all of the nation's steel mills. The President's executive order cited no specific statutory authorization, relying instead on "inherent" presidential powers allegedly vested in the President by the Constitution and "the laws of the United States." (Chester Bowles, in a characteristic New Deal attitude, had urged Truman to seize the steel industry in 1948, to prevent an increase in the price of steel—but Truman had decided not to do so.)

Taft's response was not delayed. The Taft-Hartley Act of 1947, the Selective Service Act of 1948, and the Defense Production Act of 1950 had provided procedures for settling strikes quite different from those now followed by Truman; and in none of these statutes was the seizure of property authorized; Congress had expressly rejected proposals to give the President such power as he now assumed over private property.

On April 15, Taft declared resoundingly that Truman's policy was unconstitutional. "What I object to is the President's assuming the right to seize property when there is no statutory authority for him to do so. . . . If he can seize the steel mills, I see no reason why he can't arbitrarily seize men and draft them into the Army, as he proposed to do in 1946. . . . The dangerous doctrine of inherent powers has been floating around for a good many years, but there is in fact no authority for the existence of such powers. . . . The vague theory that the President has inherent power by virtue of his office to meet a national emergency has no support in judicial decisions and runs counter to the sound and established principle that the President's authority comes simply from the provisions of the Constitution and the laws passed by Congress. . . . The Constitution says nothing about national emergencies, and if the President could increase his powers by such a declaration, there would be nothing left to the limitations largely imposed by the Constitution."[19]

Taft rejected wholly the theory of Theodore Roosevelt that the President, as "steward of the people," may do "anything that the needs of the nation demanded unless such action was forbidden by the constitution and the laws." He commended instead the interpretation of executive power offered by his father, President William Howard Taft, in *Our Chief Magistrate and His Powers*(1916). Taft concluded, "The present action of the President is in line with his general disregard of the provisions of the Constitution and laws of the United States. It follows the unjustified attempt to give the Wage Stabilization Board powers to settle disputes without complying with the provisions of Title V of the Defense Production Act. It follows the usurpation of the power to make war in Korea. It follows the usurpation of the power to send American soldiers into Korea. It is in line with the general philosophy of the New Deal and the Fair Deal, that if there is any way to avoid coming to Congress for authority to act, it will be immediately adopted. I believe that the American people are determined that we return again to a government of laws rather than a government of men."[20]

Taft judged aright. Opinion in Congress, the press, and the public generally agreed that the President had gone too far. And the Supreme Court, on June 2, handed down its decision in *Youngstown Sheet & Tube Company v. Sawyer*, 343 US 579 (1952), which ruled that the President's executive order had been illegal. For the first time since he had entered the Senate, Taft had witnessed the defeat of the Executive Force by the Supreme Court.

Congress and Foreign Affairs

Taft's campaign to restore the authority of Constitution and Congress in domestic concerns was paralleled by his endeavor to retain senatorial power in the realm of foreign affairs. Beginning in 1942, he was confronted by the expansion of presidential action in new directions—the sudden rise of executive agreements which ignored the established treaty-making provisions of the Constitution (requiring a two-thirds vote of the Senate to ratify a treaty with a foreign power).

In his speech at Aberdeen, South Dakota, in October 1942, Senator Taft strongly deplored such executive measures, as exemplified by the Atlantic Charter. "The Constitution wisely provides," he said, "that treaties must be approved by the Senate, but more and more the President is whittling away that provision of the Constitution. The Atlantic Charter was never submitted to the Senate for ratification. It is 'a joint declaration of the President of the United States and the Prime Minister . . .' They 'deem it right to make known certain common principles in the national policies of their respective countries.' Then follow various clauses expressing hopes and beliefs. In the fourth clause, however, the President purports to speak for the entire nation and to establish a policy extending many years into the future. The clause reads: 'Fourth, They will endeavor, with due respect for their existing obligations, to further the enjoyment of all states, great and small, victor and vanquished, of access, on equal terms, to the trade and to the raw materials of the world which are needed for their economic prosperity.' If this clause means what it says, it commits the United States to give every other nation access to our domestic trade. . . . Since the President did not submit it to Congress, however, it is clearly not a treaty, and I believe can do no more than express the policy of the President and his administration.[21]

Taft offered other examples of treaty-making—or the attempt at it—without senatorial approval: the twenty-six-nation agreement of January 2, 1942; the lease-lend agreements of the Secretary of State. Such agreements had been formally ratified even by the Russian Supreme Soviet; but in democratic America, the Senate had not been consulted—nor adequately informed. He said elsewhere, "The President already has tremendous power in foreign affairs, and those powers should not be extended."[22]

In the name of an amorphous international "democracy," Robert Taft believed, the genuinely democratic institutions of the United States, as expressed in representative government, were being eroded by unilateral presidential decision. The ultimate consequences might be more grave than those of the arbitrary domestic decisions of the Executive Force.

The United States and Nuremberg Justice

If arbitrary power was difficult to curb in the United States, it was harder still to observe the general principles of justice in the hard world which arose out of victory over unjust Germany, Italy, and Japan. Victors' justice was abhorrent to such a man of law as Taft; and he did not hesitate to say so, at whatever risk to his popularity and his prospects.

The United Nations Charter, he was to declare in 1949, contained no discernible principle of true justice. "Those who wrote the original draft of the United Nations Charter at Dumbarton Oaks completely forgot the ideal of justice, and even today the Charter is subject to serious criticism because it gives the Security Council power to act on grounds of expediency untempered by justice."[23] This prescient observation would take on larger significance more than a decade after Taft's death.

The rule of law must not be sacrificed to the vindictive impulse nor to prudential considerations of state. This principle led Taft to speak against the trials of Nazi leaders at Nuremberg in 1946—the most unpopular address (in the short run) he ever made. At Kenyon College, in October, shortly after the trials had ended, he participated in a conference on the heritage of the English-speaking peoples, and had for his topic "Equal Justice under Law." With an intrepidity extraordinary even in Robert Taft, he said that the accused Nazis were being tried *ex post facto*, for offenses not defined at the time they were committed. "We cannot teach liberty and justice in Germany by suppressing liberty and justice."

Should the United States participate in a "judicial" process which violated fundamental principles of Roman, English, and

American jurisprudence? "The trial of the vanquished by the victors cannot be impartial no matter how it is hedged about with the forms of justice. I question whether the hanging of those, who, however despicable, were the leaders of the German people, will ever discourage the making of aggressive war, for no one makes aggressive war unless he expects to win. About this whole judgment there is the spirit of vengeance, and vengeance is seldom justice."[24]

As Taft explained later, "My objection to the Nuremberg trials was that, while clothed with the forms of justice, they were in fact an instrument of government policy, determined months before at Teheran and Yalta."[25] In America, Taft had supported bills to prevent the lynching of Negroes; now he was not disposed to countenance the judicial lynching of Nazis, whatever their crimes. As he said at Kenyon, "The hanging of the eleven men convicted will be a blot on the American record which we shall long regret."

A wave of abuse burst upon Taft, once his remarks at Kenyon were reported in the press. The newspapers, the lawyers, and even his congressional colleagues seemed almost united against him. Such Eastern Republicans as Thomas Dewey, Irving Ives, and Jacob Javits reproached Taft; among the Democrats, Alben Barkley and Scott Lucas were ferocious in their denunciations.

But men with a real knowledge of international law and jurisprudence commended Taft. Professor Robert G. Neumann, a well-known scholar in international politics, wrote to him:

"Having spent a year in the notorious concentration camps of Dachau and Buchenwald for which these same leaders were responsible, I will hardly be suspected of pro-Nazi sympathy when I endorse your unpopular but courageous stand," he said. "None of the treaties and agreements cited by the prosecution, least of all the Kellogg-Briand Pact, were ever intended to establish individual responsibility for acts of aggression, and while the absence of such rules in international law is deeply regretted, the remedy lies with the powers who should conclude an agreement establishing a code of war crimes, and not with the courts, international or national. International law is an imperfect and incomplete body of laws. It is therefore quite inadmissible to interpret ideas no reputable international lawyer ever heard of into this body of laws by stretching civil law analogies. . . .

"The bending of the law for outright political ends is therefore bound to damage the majesty of the law and thereby undermine the foundations of our system. . . . The only precedent which has been established is the excuse of all victors to try their conquered foes. Such a principle may be convenient now, but no man can tell whether it will always remain convenient."[26]

The warmest praise of Taft's resolution came, years later, from Senator John F. Kennedy, on his rapid way to the presidency when he published *Profiles in Courage*. "He was an able politician," Kennedy wrote of Taft, "but on more than one occasion he chose to speak out in defense of a position no politician with like ambitions would have endorsed. He was, moreover, a brilliant political analyst, who knew that during his lifetime the number of American voters who agreed with the fundamental tenets of his political philosophy was destined to be a permanent minority, and that only by flattering new blocs of support—while carefully refraining from alienating any group which contained potential Taft voters—could he ever hope to attain his goal. Yet he frequently flung to the winds the very restraints his own analysis advised, refusing to bow to any group, refusing to keep silent on any issue."

Just so did Taft speak out concerning the Nuremberg Trials, Kennedy continued. In the autumn of 1946, when Taft lectured at Kenyon College, the Republicans seemed to be in a fair position to capture both houses of Congress, for the first time in two decades—which would have strongly improved Taft's prospects for the presidential nomination in 1948. "His speech exploded in the midst of a heated election campaign; and throughout the nation Republican candidates scurried for shelter while Democrats seized the opportunity to advance." Taft had foreseen this; but he was not intimidated. "Robert Taft had spoken, not in 'defense of the Nazi murderers' (as a labor leader charged), not in defense of isolationism (as most observers assumed), but in defense of what he regarded to be the traditional American concepts of law and justice."[27]

Taft refused to remain silent concerning the Nuremberg Trials because he could not in conscience ignore this fatal exercise of arbitrary power, this affront to the rule of law. "We have fooled ourselves in the belief that we could teach another nation democratic principles by force. Why, we can't even teach out own people sound principles of government," he had said in his concluding remarks at Kenyon College. "As I see it, the English-speaking peoples have one great responsibility. That is to restore to the minds of men a devotion to equal justice under law."[28]

What Taft saw at Nuremberg, indeed, was the baneful influence of legal positivism, undermining the ancient principles of justice that America had inherited from classical times and from English law. Precisely that positivism, which first had arisen in German jurisprudence, through the influence of Kelsen and other writers, had justified the totalitarian "justice" of the oligarchs whom America and her allies recently had overthrown. In the phrase of Professor John Hallowell, the legal positivists "pay lip service to liberalism, but empty liberalism of all the substantive content which it originally had. As a consequence, their 'liberalism' is more congenial to despotism than to freedom."[29]

Vexed by constitutional limitations upon the power of majorities, the legal positivists had reasoned that the rule of the law restrained the state and stood in the way of social reform. The state, they complained, was "unfree" and "a prisoner of the law," unable to act energetically for social betterment. Only by liberating the state from the abstract rule of law and from the doctrines of natural law, they argued, could forceful justice be achieved. Such positivistic concepts had spread from

Germany to Britain and the United States. Taft recognized in the political liquidation then in process at Nuremberg the juridical errors against which he had struggled in America.

The unrestrained exercise of power by democratic (and Soviet) victors could be as malignant as had been its abuse by the Nazi prisoners before the bar. Two years earlier, speaking in Indianapolis, Taft had described such a corruption of legal theory:

"Nothing is so characteristic of a totalitarian state today as the uniting of the legislative and executive functions in one man with control also over the judges. If one man can make the laws, can execute the laws, and can judge the violations of the laws, liberty cannot long exist. We may still vote once in four years, but the election becomes a mere plebiscite where the only vote is 'Ja.' The very essence of individual freedom is equal justice under a rule of law, a law to which every man shall be subject and which no executive can modify."[30]

Under the rule of law, laws ought to be general, and should not single out particular individuals; laws should be known and certain, in order that men may anticipate the consequences of their actions and act responsibly; there should be equality of law—which means not only that the laws should be applied uniformly, but also that the same laws must be applied to all. So the application of *ex post facto* laws—forbidden by the American Constitution—in the Nuremberg Trials was grossly contrary to the principle of the rule of law which the Nazis also had violated. If we hate, however righteously, without discrimination, we become like the thing we hate. Knowing that, Robert Taft found the courage to speak as he did at Kenyon College.

Taft's convictions concerning what was done at Nuremberg later were affirmed by a judge who differed with Taft in much—Justice William O. Douglas. "No matter how many books are written or briefs filed, no matter how finely the lawyers analyzed it, the crime for which the Nazis were tried had never been formalized as a crime with the definiteness required by our legal standards, nor outlawed with a death

penalty by the international community," Justice Douglas
wrote. "By our standards that crime arose under an *ex post
facto* law. Goering *et al* deserved severe punishment. But their
guilt did not justify us in substituting power for principle."[31]

The Future of Justice and Freedom

"Equal justice under law is a necessary corollary to liberty, for
there can be no liberty if the life and property of men are
subject to the arbitrary will of others," Taft wrote.[32] Those
who expected to maintain American liberties while diminishing the prescriptive rule of law, and its established forms in the
United States, were doomed to disillusion. Power unconfined
by constitution must become oppressive power.

The best protection against arbitrary coercion, he stated
often, is the maintenance of independent and impartial tri-
bunals. "Those who would destroy freedom in any country
make the courts a tool of the government, as they are in
Russia. Modern totalitarian government cannot admit the right
of any court to balk its policies."[33] For him, the development
of the American administrative commission, armed with punitive powers and ungoverned by the rules of regular courts, put
one in mind of that phrase which runs grimly through the
Soviet penal code: "by the sentence of a court of law or of an
administrative tribunal . . ." In America, the beginning might
be discerned:

"The New Deal and the present [Truman]administration
still seek the solution of every problem by the creation of
boards and commissions, with power to make regulations
having the force of law, with power to file prosecutions, try
the alleged culprits, and condemn them, practically without
recourse to the courts. Of course, in our complicated modern
system there must be some control by administrative law, as in
the fields of radio and air traffic, but it should be imposed in
such a way as to preserve the maximum amount of freedom
for those regulated; and it should subject the administrative

boards to definite principles laid down by the Congress on which an appeal can be taken to the courts. Perhaps the greatest miscarriages of justice that have ever occurred in the United States occurred under the National Labor Relations Board interpreting the Wagner Act."[34]

Some Americans thought, and think, that Taft's misgivings were unjustified by the event: the United States, they said, suffers no conspicuous reduction of liberty and justice; and so the constitutional and legal innovations of the past three decades are of no mighty significance. Yet a sentence of David Hume's deserves repetition: "It is seldom that liberty of any kind is lost all at once."

Notes, CHAPTER V

1. John F. Kennedy, *Profiles in Courage* (Memorial Edition New York, 1964), p. 243.
2. T. V. Smith and Robert A. Taft, *Foundations of Democracy* (New York, 1939), pp. 37, 21.
3. *Ibid.*, pp. 27–28.
4. *Ibid.*, pp. 24–28.
5. Robert A. Taft, "Sidestepping the Constitution," *The Review of Reviews*, Vol. XCIV, No. 3 (September 1936), p. 34 ff.
6. Smith and Taft, *Foundations of Democracy, op. cit.*, p. 56.
7. For serious examination of the actual and potential powers of Congress, see Alfred de Grazia, *Republic in Crisis: Congress against the Executive Force* (New York, 1965); and James Burnham, *Congress and the American Tradition* (Chicago, 1959).
8. Roland Young, *Congressional Politics in the Second World War* (New York, 1956), p. 219.
9. Robert A. Taft, "A New Order after the War," speech before the Ohio State Bar Association at Toledo, October 24,

1941; printed in the *Congressional Record*, 77th Congress, 1st Session, Vol. 87, Part 14 (October 27, 1941), p. A4837.

10. Robert A. Taft, "What about Congress?," radio address over Station WGAR, Cleveland, August 8, 1942; printed in the *Congressional Record*, 77th Congress, 2nd Session, Vol. 88, Part 10 (August 10, 1942), pp. A3055–A3056.

11. Robert A. Taft, "The Job of the 78th Congress," speech delivered before the Akron Junior Chamber of Commerce, January 28, 1943; printed in the *Congressional Record*, 78th Congress, 1st Session, Vol. 89, Part 9 (February 1, 1943), p. A365.

12. *Ibid.*, pp. A366–A367.

13. Robert A. Taft, "We Need a Courageous and Independent Congress," speech delivered at Aberdeen, South Dakota, October 12, 1942; printed in the *Congressional Record*, 78th Congress, 1st Session, 1943, Vol. 89, Part 9 (January 7, 1943), pp. A32–A33.

14. Reported in *The New York Times*, July 10, 1943, p. 36.

15. *Ibid.*

16. Robert A. Taft, "Compulsory Military Training in Peacetime Will Destroy Government by the People," speech delivered at Gettysburg National Cemetery, May 30, 1945; printed in the *Congressional Record*, 79th Congress, 1st Session, Vol. 91, Part 11 (May 31, 1945), p. A2609.

17. Quoted in Young, *Congressional Politics, op. cit.*, pp. 94–95.

18. Young, *op. cit.*, p. 95.

19. Robert A. Taft, "Seizure of the Steel Industry," speech delivered in Pittsburgh, April 15, 1952; printed in the *Congressional Record*, 82nd Congress, 2nd Session, Vol. 98, Part 3 (April 16, 1952), pp. 4014–4015.

20. *Ibid.*

21. Taft, "We Need a Courageous and Independent Congress," *op. cit.*, p. A34.

22. Reported in *The New York Times*, December 3, 1942, p. 1.

23. Robert A. Taft, "The Republican Party," *Fortune*, Vol. XXXIX, No. 4 (April 1949), p. 114.

24. Robert A. Taft, "Liberty and Justice for the Individual," address at Kenyon College, Gambier, Ohio, October 1946; printed in *The Heritage of the English-Speaking Peoples and their Responsibility* (Kenyon College, Gambier, Ohio, 1947); also printed in *Vital Speeches*, Vol. 13, No. 2 (November 1, 1946), p. 47, under the title "Equal Justice under Law."

25. Taft, "The Republican Party," *op. cit.*, pp. 114, 116.

26. Robert G. Neumann to Robert A. Taft, October 5, 1946. Robert A. Taft Papers, Library of Congress.

27. Kennedy, *Profiles in Courage, op. cit.*, pp. 232, 233, 243.

28. Taft, "Liberty and Justice for the Individual," *op. cit.*, pp. 168–169.

29. John Hallowell, *Main Currents in Modern Political Thought* (New York, 1950), p. 358.

30. Robert A. Taft, "Usurpation of Power by the Executive Branch," speech before the Republican Editorial Association, Indianapolis, Indiana, March 11, 1944; printed in the *Congressional Record*, 78th Congress, 2nd Session, Vol. 90, Part 8 (March 13, 1944), p. A1258.

31. Quoted in Kennedy, *Profiles in Courage, op. cit.*, pp. 236–237.

32. Taft, "The Republican Party," *Fortune, op. cit.*, p. 114.

33. *Ibid.*

34. *Ibid.*, p. 116.

CHAPTER VI

Organized Labor and the Public Interest

Justice, Power, and American Labor

A JUST MAN: in a phrase, that is the American public's strongest impression of Robert Taft, fourteen years after his death.
The classical principle of justice is to accord to every man his
due. The legislator's task is to ensure that interests and individuals in the commonwealth enjoy the rights and rewards
which should be theirs—and to prevent interests and individuals from encroaching upon the rights and rewards of
others. The just state maintains a balance of claims and powers,
that general justice may be attained.

In seeking to achieve justice in the relationships of labor
unions, of industrial management and ownership, and of the
public interest, Taft made his most enduring positive contribution to the American political structure. In those years, disturbed though most members of Congress were by violent
labor disputes, few relished the prospect of belling the cat.
Complex new legislation would require unusual practical talents in the authors of such bills—and intrepidity; yet the great
unions scarcely would be grateful. Nevertheless, in the event,
Taft's labor legislation made him more popular than did anything else in his political life—probably to his own surprise,
and despite the abuse heaped upon his work by labor-union
leaders.

For Taft, as for the Federalists in the Republic's early years, one high merit of the federal system was its efficacy in checking and balancing the principal interests in society. No single interest must be permitted to prevail against the common welfare; and in large part, the Constitution was an instrument to prevent such aggrandizement by strong groups. Of aggressive interests in Taft's own time, the most powerful was organized labor.

Labor unions, Taft believed, were necessary and in many ways socially beneficial; they must not be injured, nor must workingmen be neglected or oppressed. When the legitimate prerogatives and claims of labor were in danger, therefore, Taft stood on labor's side, with strong effect—as when President Truman attempted to conscript striking railwaymen. But when organized labor, ignoring the general public interest, denied to management and ownership their lawful functions and rewards, and treated arbitrarily its own membership, federal authority was required to restore balance in the commonwealth—and so Taft wrote the Taft-Hartley Act. His object throughout was to restore the balance of the scales of justice.

During Taft's years in politics, the recovery of balance meant ordinarily that the claims of the labor-union leaders must be restrained. Before the Roosevelt era, it had been otherwise. So late as 1930, only four million Americans had belonged to labor unions; the high-handed ways of many employers, the company blacklist, the "yellow-dog contract," and similar practices had roused strong justified resentment among crowds of industrial workers. Before 1935, the case had been strong for redress to American labor.

In the first years of the New Deal, the balance of justice had been radically altered by the passage and operation of the Norris-LaGuardia Act and the Wagner Act. In general, Taft approved of those reforms. But a tardy redress, adopted in a time of violent protest, often goes beyond necessity or justice: as Tocqueville puts the principle, "Halfway down the stairs, we threw ourselves out of the window in order to reach the ground more quickly." In questions of labor, the scales of commutative justice had sunk down too far on the other side. One eminent early New Dealer, Donald Richberg, himself an author of the Norris-LaGuardia Act, has summarized the consequences of excessive governmental intervention in favor of unions, during the Roosevelt era:

"The Wagner Act established a strong labor protective list of 'unfair practices' by employers; but it took no account of protecting employers from the equally obvious and harmful 'unfair practices' of labor. It tied the employers down against even advocating their side of labor disputes while granting a sweeping license to the unions. The enormous injury to a free economy which was engendered by the act became soon evident when its administration was undertaken by a crew of zealots who openly admitted that they conceived their function to be to help organized labor turn collective bargaining into collective coercion and assume a dominant role in industry."[1]

The haste with which unions had grown after passage of the Wagner Act, moreover, had opened the way to other abuses. Before and during the Second World War, ominous Communist penetration occurred in some important unions; small independent unions were pushed to the wall by the Congress of Industrial Organizations and—to a smaller extent—by the American Federation of Labor; labor racketeers obtained mastery over other unions; and the violent tactics of many union bosses, in the years of the "goon squad," subjected some industrial employees to a regime more arbitrary and dangerous than they had known before the Roosevelt reforms. By judicial decisions, unions had been exempted from the operation of antitrust laws, even though some people influential in the Roosevelt administration—notably Thurman Arnold—believed that this exemption must bring with it dangers of monopoly and inflation.

The unions' political power, mightily increasing, deterred many members of Congress from directly opposing union claims; from union exhortation and union treasuries came, directly or indirectly, funds to finance political campaigns or to produce political propaganda which, in some states, distinctly exceeded the contributions of businessmen and others whose interests squinted another way. It was not altogether safe for a politician to assert against such a new concentration of power the general public interest.

But Robert Taft set himself to redress this disturbed balance; and in considerable part, he succeeded. If he had failed, legislation much more tightly restricting union activities might have been enacted, during his time in Congress or later; or, alternatively, the unions might have grown insufferably arrogant and politically uncontrollable, with proportionate injury to the economy, the public interest, and private rights. With this background, Taft's labor policies before 1947 must be examined.

An Enemy of Labor?

Even before the day of the Taft-Hartley Act, union propagandists and many liberal publicists endeavored to persuade the electorate that Taft was "a tool of big business"—or, at best, a politician indifferent to the welfare of the poor and of organized labor because insulated against privation by his affluence; even those who conceded that he was a man of honest convictions sometimes argued that his nature was unfeeling. An inspection of Taft's circumstances and record does not sustain these views.

Although Taft possessed private means sufficient to secure his political independence of either business or labor, his was not one of the great American fortunes; his private income was on the scale of Adlai Stevenson's, among the Democrats, or somewhat less. His grandfather had left only five thousand dollars, including a house; and his father also had not accumulated a really great capital. "The Taft inheritance might be briefly stated to comprise an old house, much out of repair, a great deal of furniture and silver, and very little else."[2]

Another branch of the family was wealthy; Robert Taft made a very good income from practice of the law, before devoting himself to national politics; and the family's thrifty habits and well-considered investments lifted Taft (though he never was worth more than a half-million dollars) above dependence on any financial or political set. But in an age of millionaires, he had no vast resources; nor did he ever receive massive financial support, during his campaigns, from "Wall Street" or any other part of the business community; indeed, his successive rivals for the Republican presidential nomination, and the Democratic occupants of the White House, all were better buoyed up by millionaire political backers, and more strongly supported by corporate favor or by union contributions.

The charge that Taft did not "understand the common man" because of his old family name and his private means becomes sufficiently absurd if one considers the case of Franklin Roosevelt, a politician considerably richer, of a family no less well known, and more aristocratic in personality than was the Senator from Ohio; nor are Harrimans, Rockefellers, and Kennedys generally considered by the liberal press to be devoid of human sympathies, despite their immense means. Taft's attitudes concerning labor questions, and social reform generally, were founded upon personal conviction and party principle, not upon class interest or class indifference.

Nor was Taft hostile toward organized labor: he declined to dance to the tune called by various labor-union leaders, but the true interests of union members had no better defender. As a member of the Ohio legislature, Taft supported many measures endorsed by the unions. He voted, for instance, to establish a commission to study minimum wages for women and minors; twice he advocated bills for workmen's compensation; he worked for ratification of the proposed child-labor amendment to the federal Constitution, supported a bill requiring that convict-made products be so labeled, and backed a bill to prohibit "yellow dog" labor contracts.

In the United States Senate, Taft's first vote on a labor question was in support of Senator La Follette's bill to prohibit the use of labor spies, professional strike-breakers, and firearms in labor disputes. But he was resolved not to grant to the unions power that would injure the commonwealth. During his first year in the Senate, Taft wrote to Henry Pringle, the biographer of William Howard Taft, explaining his father's and his own convictions on labor questions. President Taft, his son declared, held as the firmest of all his convictions the belief "that law enforcement, law and order, was the first essential of civilization. He believed that if respect and compliance with law was ever broken down it would destroy all the benefits of civilization, including those of workmen as well as everybody else. This is the key to his violent feeling about the Pullman Strike."

His father had been right to oppose the secondary boycott, Taft continued; and that labor weapon had become more destructive of justice and the public interest since the National Labor Relations Board had attained power. "The situation in the Pacific lumber industry is unbearable. Lumber produced by CIO plants is boycotted by AF of L carpenters. Lumber produced in AF of L plants is boycotted by CIO longshoremen, and the export market has been wiped out—though all the producers have obeyed the NLRB certifications. I have no doubt that if the subject of the rights of labor is ever dealt with by legislation the secondary boycott will be outlawed, and labor will not greatly object."[3] (Eight years later, Senator Taft's own bill would accomplish just that.)

It was not so much Taft's direct policy toward labor unions, before 1947, which brought him into conflict with the union leaders, as it was the unions' thorough support for the whole Roosevelt program. Most union leaders confounded opposition to the New Deal with hostility toward organized labor, and planned political retaliation accordingly. As early as 1944, Ohio labor leaders fought hard to defeat Taft's candidacy for a second term in the Senate, even though his record was scarcely anti-union. A CIO tract was entitled "He Wanted to Do Business with Hitler and Hirohito: The Amazing Story of Senator Taft." Its title was more moderate than its text, for this pamphlet denounced "This shrewd, calculating tory, who influences American government from his post as chairman of the Republican steering committee of the U.S. Senate." Taft's alleged wealth was held against him, and the anonymous pamphleteer implied that Taft was a Fascist, whose opposition to Roosevelt's foreign policy was virtual treason.[4]

In 1945, Taft further vexed union leaders by opposing Roosevelt's "Economic Bill of Rights"—especially its utopian guarantee of perpetual "full employment," as a matter of right, to everybody under all circumstances. The union spokesmen had embraced this proposal enthusiastically; Taft would have no part of it.

"We can all agree that full employment at good wages for every man and every woman who wishes to work in the United States is a goal devoutly to be wished," Taft told the National Industrial Conference Board. "It is an ideal strenuously to be sought, and no questioning of its existence as a legal right in any way detracts from the desire of the questioner to attain the ideal." But it could not be an absolute right; that notion was impractical. The Declaration of Independence "mentions only the rights to life, liberty, and the pursuit of happiness. The Constitution, while promising to secure the blessings of liberty, only proposes to promote the general welfare." A guarantee of work would be impossible to fulfill, and was "wholly inconsistent with the very freedom which has produced and animated the machine which provides jobs at good wages."

President Roosevelt, and the Congress of Industrial Organizations which backed this proposal, had talked of guaranteeing fifty or sixty million jobs. But, Taft inquired, "What is full employment and what is a good wage? Is there to be a guarantee of any job a man wants in any industry, or is it to be such a job as the Government chooses to provide? . . . The President says every man has the right to a job in the 'industries or shops or farms or mines of the nation.' The total number of men employed in these categories is only thirty million. How can they be increased and why should they be? . . . It is clear to me that any direct guarantee of full-time jobs at good wages would involve the Government in the placement of every man and woman in the country, and ultimately the assignment by the Government of every man and woman to the job selected by the Government. This is exactly the system pursued in Russia today."[5]

Taft's other arguments in this speech demonstrated that the concept of full employment could be realized only in a socialist state—and even there only at the cost of diminished production and of total direction of labor; it would be fatal to the character of the people, and contrary to the material interest of every wage-earner. At that time, however, this scheme (which subsequently never went further than an unenforced and unenforceable declaratory act) was dear to the hearts of Walter Reuther and his colleagues in the CIO, and they took Taft for their most effective enemy.

The union leaders, or most of them, ignored Taft's strong support, during this period, for a variety of measures favored by the labor unions. In 1944, for example, Taft voted against Vandenberg's amendment to the Revenue Act, which would have required labor unions to file income-tax returns for 1943. In 1946, he voted to increase the minimum wage in interstate commerce from forty to sixty cents an hour. These were not the marks of an "enemy of labor." And in the spring of 1946, he was to become the successful champion of unionists against the arbitrary power of government.

The Freedom of Labor and the Railroad Strike

In 1941, both unions and management had promised to abstain from strikes or lock-outs for the duration of the war. But as military victory approached, many unions announced that they would press for large wage increases, and that they no longer considered themselves bound by their no-strike pledges. With the relaxing of wage controls by 1945, the unions felt confident of achieving substantial increases, despite wage ceilings established during the war.

So, late in 1945, a wave of strikes washed over the American economy: the automobile, steel, electrical, and meat-packing industries were worst affected. In some instances, President Truman's requests for compromise were defied openly by union leaders, especially in mining and the railways. John L. Lewis, head of the United Mine Workers, infuriated Truman when he refused to halt a national coal strike, even though the government (under the Smith-Connally Act, a war-time measure) had taken control of the mines. The railroads also were seized, for a brief time, by the government. In the spring of 1946, the railroad Brotherhoods rejected a proposal by a fact-finding board for a wage-increase of sixteen cents an hour; in May, Brotherhood leaders called a strike of more than 250,000 railroad workers.

At the President's request, the strike was postponed during further negotiations. The union leaders originally had justified the strike by their need for an eighteen-cent hourly wage increase, and for forty-five changes in working rules. But during the further negotiations, five days after the original demand, the unions rejected an increase of eighteen and a half cents, coupled with a proposal of management that rules changes be delayed for one year. On May 23, the Brotherhoods ordered a strike on 337 railroads, involving more than 350,000 employees.

President Truman's patience, never durable, now gave way. On May 24, Truman announced that the strike was in defiance of the federal government; he ordered the strikers back to work, saying that he would call on the army, otherwise, within twenty-four hours. That evening, the President addressed the nation by radio; on May 25, he spoke to a joint session of Congress, demanding immediate enactment of an emergency bill to give him power to conscript into the armed forces all striking railwaymen. The attorney-general would be empowered to obtain special injunctions, recalcitrant railwaymen would lose rights of seniority, and criminal penalities would be provided for defiant Brotherhood leaders.

The House of Representatives, with a Democratic majority, alarmed at the prospect of the collapse of rail transportation, debated this proposal only one hour—and then passed the President's bill by a majority of 306 to 11. Alben Barkley, majority leader, promptly asked unanimous consent that the bill be made the immediate business of the Senate.

In this exigency, Senator Taft rose with his usual self-possession and called the President's bill ridiculous. A few Democratic and Republican senators promptly joined him in opposition—among them, such liberals as Pepper and Morse.

The majority leadership hesitated; debate was continued until Monday, May 27. Tempers having cooled by that time, the more startling features of the bill were deleted. On May 29, the section authorizing the President to draft strikers was defeated by the surprising vote of seventy to nineteen—Taft's remarkable work of persuasion. Even Senator Barkley was converted to opposition; and by voice vote, Barkley passed another amendment, striking out provisions that would have deprived the railwaymen of seniority rights.

For Taft, this attempt to coerce the railway Brotherhoods by an abrupt exercise of military authority was arbitrary power incarnate, denying the rule of law and the concept of due process; also, if established as a precedent, it would have given the President virtually unlimited—and unpredictable—power over the economy, to be exercised without plan and without regular principles of justice. And labor unions that must yield instanter to a threat of military conscription, he knew, soon would cease to be free or responsible.

Though the emasculated bill was sent back to the House, the House Rules Committee took no action, and Truman's emergency measure never reached a conference committee. The rule of law, and Robert Taft, had prevailed once more.

This affair was one of the more interesting exhibitions of Taft's mastery of parliamentary tactics in the cloakrooms, and of the art of persuasion in Congress, on or off the floor. It is no

wonder that this was the year when Taft's senatorial colleagues named him as the most effective member of the Senate.
But Taft's victory over Truman was more than a clever
piece of political management: it was an act of statecraft. Taft
had prevented the enacting of a precedent which might have
crippled labor unions; yet the union leaders contrived to
forget Taft's stand, soon enough—as did Harry Truman. In
his *Memoirs*, Truman was to write that his bill had meant
drastic measures. "They were against the principles I believed
in, and I proposed them only as a desperate resort in an
extreme emergency where leaders defiantly called the workers
out in a strike against the Government."[6] Truman does not
refer to Taft's part in the controversy—nor does he acknowledge that it was Taft who saved Truman from the hasty
violation of his own principles.

Even while Truman's reaction to the railroad strike was at
its peppery height, the Senate was passing the Case Bill, an
abortive forerunner of the Taft-Hartley Act. The Case Bill was
meant to empower the government to deal with strikes that
menaced the national interest, and to redress the balance of the
Wagner Act. In the spring of 1946, President Truman vetoed
the Case Bill, and Congress sustained his veto; yet it had
become clear that the majority in both Senate and House
demanded new legislation to exercise some restraint upon the
power of unions.

The Taft-Hartley Act was an intelligent response to this
congressional and public demand for reform in labor-management relations. Before turning to Taft's most enduring piece
of legislation, it is necessary to examine the background.

The Taft-Hartley Act

Of the Labor Relations Act of 1935 (the Wagner Act),
Robert Taft approved, on several counts. This Wagner Act
had guaranteed to labor unions the right to collective bargaining, with freedom from influence by employers. It had speci-

fied unfair labor practices, and had forbidden employers to resort to these: employers might not influence labor unions, nor discriminate against union members and individual employees, nor refuse to bargain collectively. Workers were guaranteed the right to organize and join unions, to bargain collectively with employers through their unions, and to strike. The act was to be enforced by the National Labor Relations Board. No provision had been made for restraining unfair practices by unions, nor for governmental intervention to avert an immense strike or lockout injurious to the public interest.

During his earlier years in the Senate, Taft did not object strongly to the advantage which the Wagner Act gave to the unions, nor to the lack of provision for maintaining the public interest during an emergency. His criticism was concerned, rather, with the administration of the act by the National Labor Relations Board, whose members from the beginning had been emphatically inclined toward the unions' side, and who rapidly had arrogated powers not contemplated, or at least not specified, by Congress, when the Wagner Act was ratified. In his first campaign for the Senate, Taft had pointed out the prejudices of the NLRB, and during his first year in the Senate had continued this sharp criticism, asking that the members of the existing Board be dismissed and that persons more nearly impartial be appointed to their places. He also had recommended, in 1939, amendments to the Wagner Act—that company unions be forbidden; that employers be permitted to express preference among competing unions; that craft unions be allowed freedom of choice when confronted with domination by one of the big new "horizontal" unions; that labor elections be governed by specific regulations; that the judicial functions of the NLRB be separated from its prosecuting functions.

As Sylvester Petro comments, the Supreme Court (going beyond Congress's intention) had "adopted a jurisprudential principle according to which the National Labor Relations Board, a quasi-judicial agency in the executive branch of government, was largely freed of judicial control in applying the already pro-union Wagner Law in disputes between unions and employers. At the same time, in the opinion of many, the purely executive branch of government was likewise favorably disposed toward the large labor unions. By acts of the President himself, the Department of Labor, and the National Labor Relations Board, the weight and prestige of the executive department were thrown usually on the side of the unions in labor disputes, although the usual formalities of nonpartisanship were observed and even perfected."[7]

Congressional resentment at this tendency, and at its consequences in the arrogance of union leaders, increased steadily. The strikes which followed the Second World War turned congressional and public opinion further still toward amendment of the Wagner Act. The grim prospect of a national railroad strike gave the Case Bill impetus almost sufficient to secure its enactment in the teeth of President Truman's opposition.

In 1947, with the convening of the Eightieth Congress, Truman perceived that both houses were ready to act decisively and thoroughly on labor questions. Truman resisted no longer—or, rather, he prepared to make concessions. In his State of the Union message, the President asked Congress to amend the Wagner Act by prohibiting jurisdictional strikes (caused by disputes between rival unions), certain types of secondary boycotts, and strikes over conflicting interpretations of existing contracts with management; also he recommended legislation to improve methods of labor mediation, and to provide for voluntary arbitration and fact-finding boards. Making a virtue of necessity, Senator Claude Pepper— a chief congressional spokesman for the unions—declared that these principles were acceptable; Senator Wagner expected that Congress would do as the President wished.

Robert Taft, the new chairman of the Senate Labor Committee, smiled as he commented that President Truman "seems to have accepted about one-half of the Case bill, which he vetoed last May, and the same portion of the Republican proposals just made in the Ball bill, and not to have ruled out the rest of these measures."⁸ But Truman did not ask for enough; and the Republicans, fortified by Taft's knowledge of labor-management problems, prepared to pass their own bill.

In close cooperation with the House Labor Committee (the chairman of which was Representative Fred A. Hartley, of New Jersey), the Senate Labor Committee, under Taft's leadership, set to work. The Hartley Bill was passed by the House on April 19; the Taft Bill by the Senate, on the same day. It was obvious that from a Senate-House conference committee would emerge a bill which, whether vetoed by the President or not, would become law.

In appointing senators to the conference committee, Senator Taft selected men representing views to both the right and the left of his own—as, earlier, he had encouraged the appointment of liberal Republicans to his Labor Committee; he desired broad support for the new legislation. The amendments to the Wagner Act were aimed not at labor generally, Taft said, but at the union bosses: "A large part of this bill is devoted to giving individual employees a little more freedom from the orders of labor union officials."⁹

President Truman did veto the bill; but the House overrode his veto by a majority of three hundred and thirty-one to eighty-three, the Senate by sixty-eight to twenty-five, on June 20 and June 23, 1947. The National Labor-Management Relations Act, or Taft-Hartley Act, became the law of the land.

This Taft-Hartley Act retained the definitions of management's "unfair practices" forbidden by the Wagner Act. But to restore the balance between labor and management, and to safeguard the public interest, the new Act specified and forbade a series of unfair labor practices on the part of unions. It also provided for action in the event of strikes causing national emergencies: the President was authorized to order the suspension of a strike for eighty days, should the national health or safety be endangered, in time of war or of peace.

Senator Taft's reform was a complex piece of legislation, and what summary can be made of it here is not wholly adequate; those interested in its details should read the text of the Act, with the aid of a legal commentary.* Among its many sections, however, the following important provisions were made for greater freedom and responsibility in labor-management relations:

1. Unions might not restrain or coerce employees in the right to join, or to refuse to join, any union.

2. Unions might not restrain or coerce workers in the exercise of the right to bargain collectively through representatives of their own choosing.

3. Unions might not interfere with an employer in choosing his representatives for collective bargaining or for the adjustment of grievances.

4. Unions might not bar a worker from employment because he had been denied union membership for any reason except non-payment of dues or fees, or in violation of provisions prohibiting the closed shop.

5. Unions might not attempt to coerce an employer to discriminate against an employee, in violation of the open-shop provisions of this act.

6. Unions might not require, under a permitted union shop, any initiation fee regarded as excessive or discriminatory by the National Labor Relations Board.

7. Unions might not refuse to bargain collectively with an employer, when the union should be the certified bargaining agent.

8. Unions might not engage in strikes to force an employer or a self-employed person to join the union; to effect a secondary boycott; to compel an employer, through a "sym-

* The Taft-Hartley Act, the Case Bill, and President Truman's proposed labor legislation are summarized, with some background information, in Chapter 5, "Labor," of *Congress and the Nation, 1945–1964: A Review of Government and Politics in the Postwar Years* (Washington: Congressional Quarterly Service, 1965). See particularly pp. 580–584. For useful general studies in this field, with some comments on the Taft-Hartley Act, see *The Public Stake in Union Power*, edited by Philip D. Bradley (Charlottesville, Virginia, 1959); *Compulsory Arbitration and Government Intervention in Labor Disputes*, by Herbert R. Northrup (Washington, 1966); *Union Monopolies and Antitrust Restraints*, by Patrick M. Boarman (Washington, 1965).

pathy" strike or boycott, to recognize one union when another already had been certified as bargaining agent; to force, through jurisdictional strikes and boycotts, an employer to assign work to members of some particular union instead of another.

9. Unions might not force employers to pay for work not performed or intended (a reduction of union "featherbedding").

10. Suits against unions for breach of contract were authorized.

11. Union shops (allowing firms to hire union or non-union workers for a specified period—usually a month—before all employees should be required to join the union) were authorized—provided that the union shop was not prohibited by state laws. These union shops must be agreed to by a majority of the employees, voting by secret ballot, and the union must be certified by the NLRB. Closed shops (which require that an employee must join the union before being engaged by the employer) were prohibited, although they had been permitted under the Wagner Act.

12. Unions would be denied the countenance and protection of the NLRB unless they should file with the Department of Labor various financial reports and copies of their constitutions and by-laws, and unless all of their officers should file affidavits that they were not Communists, Communist sympathizers, or members of any group believing in the overthrow of the government by force.

13. Employees and employers, under a "free speech" provision, were allowed to express their views on unions, if they implied no threats or promises of benefits.

14. Written authorization from union members, on an annual basis, was required to permit the union dues-checkoff system.

15. The National Labor Relations Board was reorganized, being increased from three members to five, and limited to the exercise of judicial functions. A special General Counsel to the Board was to be appointed by the President, to investigate

complaints and to bring them before the Board for determination. Unless the General Counsel should issue a formal complaint in a case of alleged unfair labor practices, the Board could take no action; and the General Counsel was authorized to seek injunctions under certain provisions of the act.

A prodigious amount of investigation and consultation had been undertaken by Taft for the preparation of this elaborate statute. By its moderation, it was calculated to attract much support from both parties in Congress and in the nation; many politicians of liberal leanings voted for it; indeed, such a piece of legislation was long overdue, but only Taft's advancement to the headship of the Senate Labor Committee had made enactment possible against Presidential opposition. It took away no one's real rights; instead, it conferred new rights— and not merely upon employers, but upon employees, both union members and independent workers.

Despite the fulminations of President Truman, Senator Pepper, and most labor-union officials, the Taft-Hartley Act would not be undone. And neither would its principal author, as a force in national politics, whatever the union leaders might contrive against him; for the Act was received with relief and praise by the business community, the majority of adherents of either party, and the greater part of the unions' membership —if covertly, by these last. It was eminently a just act, applied to grievances that had cried out for redress.

Successful Defense of the Taft-Hartley Act

By September 1947, the Act was working well, and Senator Taft said at Santa Cruz, in California, "It is silly to talk about a 'slave labor bill' when the first settlement made under that bill was one which increased the wages of coal miners by more than 30 per cent."[10] In March, 1948, Taft reviewed in *Collier's* the operation of his law:

"I think it is fair to say that nearly all of the many amendments made to existing labor laws by the new act have worked satisfactorily to promote justice between employers and employees and between labor union leaders and their members. At the same time greater protection has been given to the public, and the number of strikes has decreased. . . . The Wagner Act made it easy for employees to obtain representation by a union. They merely voted for the union at a government-conducted election. If the union proved unsatisfactory, however, the only way for the employees to get rid of it was to vote in another union. The NLRB refused to recognize a petition of 'no' union. We were assured by the union leaders that it was only the employers who ever wanted to discharge the union as bargaining agent. . . . Apparently the union leaders were wrong. Statistical releases by NLRB at the end of the first 60 days of operation under the new statute disclosed that 18 per cent of the petitions for elections were filed by employees to obtain decertification of the union that had been representing them. . . . It must be remembered that the new act in no way interferes with the right of men to strike for better hours, wages, or working conditions. It is based entirely on free collective bargaining, which means that if an agreement cannot be reached there may be no work done."

He repeated, in this article, his defense of the right to strike: "Most of the public seems to feel that strikes should be prohibited by law. They do not realize that if strikes are prohibited some means must be found to fix a fair wage by arbitration or otherwise. That means in the long run the government must appoint the arbitrators and must finally assume the responsibility of fixing a wage pattern. If the government fixes wages, the argument for fixing prices cannot be fairly met. If prices are fixed it means rationing and complete control of distribution. That is the end of a free economy."[11]

From its inception, the Taft-Hartley Act was popular with the general public. The Republican defeat in the autumn elections of 1948 brought Democratic majorities to Senate and House; but President Truman was unable to obtain from his

Democratic Congress the repeal or modification of the Act. In the Senate and out of it, Taft skillfully defended his legislation. The only changes which the Senate of the Eighty-first Congress approved were improvements recommended by Taft himself—although those Taft amendments failed to pass the House.

In subsequent years, Taft endeavored to make minor improvements in his Act, but no important amendment was approved by Congress until 1959, when the Landrum-Griffin Act added provisions to diminish criminality, coercion, and fraud within unions. Repeated vigorous attempts by union leaders to repeal most of the Act, or to have it declared unconstitutional, got nowhere; in 1966, a Congress dominated by Democrats of liberal inclination declined to repeal Section 14*b* of the Act, which authorized states to enact right-to-work laws.

The question remained, during the first three years of this law's operation, whether its architect could survive the bitter resentment of the masters of the labor movement. In Washington, the Act and his other economic and social legislation about this time had added to his reputation: in 1949, a poll of Washington press correspondents and radio commentators, assessing the abilities of members of the Senate, ranked Taft highest in that body for "contributing most to the country's welfare" and being the "most conscientious" senator. But the union leaders had declared that they would unseat him.

In 1950, Taft stood for re-election; and the big unions flung into that contest their formidable resources. Defamatory pamphlets were scattered broadcast about Ohio by the labor organizations; five unions combined to distribute a million copies of a comic book meant to ruin Taft. The vituperative character of this general assault seems to have gained a substantial sympathy vote for the Republican candidate—who was alleged, in a "Speaker's Handbook" against Taft published by the Congress of Industrial Organizations, to have "defended employer spy systems and wanted employers left free to pile up arsenals of tear gas, riot guns, and other munitions."

This was bathos, and the Ohio electorate knew it. To judge from election returns in industrial constituencies, union members recognized the falsity of the accusations, too. Robert Taft was re-elected by a margin of four hundred thousand votes, the greatest majority he ever obtained. Although some other factors were involved in his victory, his labor legislation had been vindicated in his own state.

An Enduring Work of Equity

"Though it has been said a thousand times that Taft set out simply in a punitive frame of mind and with a spirit of vengeance (the political action committees of labor having long since made him a favorite antagonist) it is my belief that any bystander who saw the whole Taft-Hartley business unfold would not accept this charge." So William S. White wrote, in 1954.[12] Today, comparatively few would argue that Taft wrote his Act as a punitive measure. The Taft-Hartley Act may be improved, but it will not be abandoned.

Reasoned criticism in recent years, indeed, tends toward the view that the Act did not go far enough to redress the balance in labor relationships and to ensure adequate consideration of the public interest. In part, the intention of the Act has been altered by the re-interpretations of the National Labor Relations Board; and, far from making the labor unions servile, the Act has not changed gravely the preference given to the labor unions, over management, by the Wagner Act, nor kept the federal government totally impartial. Roscoe Pound points out that it remains difficult to hold unions responsible for breach of contract, despite the Taft-Hartley provisions, and that the employer still suffers from heavy burdens in law:

"In fact, employer and union are by no means on an equality under the amendments made by the Taft-Hartley Act. The employer is held for what his agents and employees do in the course of their employment. The union is not held for what is done under its aegis by its members. We are told the union leaders avow a belief that actions for damages may be utilized to destroy local unions. The unions are to be guarded 'against a potentially crushing liability.' No one else has protection against liability for wrong-doing lest it crush him financially. A manufacturer can be put in bankruptcy by having to pay for wrongs done third persons by negligence of his employees.

"The claim of the unions under the National Labor Relatons Act to be the favorite of the government and to be exempt from equality before the law is not much impaired in practical result by the Taft-Hartley Act. Restrictions upon the activities of employers in labor relations are given the backing of administrative enforcement by a board set up specially for the purpose, provided with ample machinery for its tasks, and fortified by power given the federal courts to enforce the board's orders by injunctions and proceedings for contempt. There is no comparable machinery of enforcement on the employer's side."[13]

It has been objected, too, that the Taft-Hartley Act cannot suffice to secure the public interest, in prolonged emergency, if unions should be obdurate; for its "cooling-off period" must expire, in such circumstances, without a strike having been terminated. But no one has proposed an alternative to this provision satisfactory to Congress.

However that may be, Robert Taft restored a large measure of order and justice to industrial relations; many of the excesses of the less responsible or less honest of labor leaders have been diminished by his Act, and the great wheel of circulation has been able to revolve in a tolerable way; while an injudicious reaction against labor unions has been averted. In this field, more than in any other, Taft proved himself to be a true statesman.

"The Taft-Hartley Act was written for only one purpose—to establish justice and equality in labor-management relations," Taft said in March 1948. "Such justice and equality is absolutely essential if we are to find the way to capital-labor peace, as justice in international affairs is the key to world peace. It is not a new law, but a revision of elaborate existing laws, such as the Wagner Act and the Norris-La Guardia Act, which were so one-sided that they conferred on labor union leaders arbitrary powers over all but the largest employers, and, even more important, over their own members. . . . The revision of the law was not inspired by any idea of vengeance or any prejudice against labor unions. The committee which reported the bill was largely pro-labor, and the pro-labor members took the position that labor itself would be benefited by a correction of the abuses which had arisen."[14]

Two decades later, those remarks almost have ceased to be controversial.

Notes, CHAPTER VI

1. Donald Richberg, *Labor Union Monopoly: a Clear and Present Danger* (Chicago, 1957), pp. 37–39.

2. See Helen Taft Manning, "My Brother Bob Taft," *The American Magazine*, Vol. CLIII, No. 1 (January 1952), p. 102. Considerable information about the Taft background will be found in Ishbel Ross, *An American Family: the Tafts, 1678 to 1964.* (Cleveland and New York, 1964).

3. Robert A. Taft to Henry F. Pringle, August 31, 1939. Pringle Papers, Library of Congress.

4. Copy in Robert A. Taft Papers, Library of Congress.

5. Robert A. Taft, "Guaranty of Full-Time Employment at Standard Wages," address delivered to the National Industrial Conference Board in New York City, January 18, 1945; printed in the *Congressional Record*, 79th Congress, 1st Session, Vol. 91, Part 10 (January 22, 1945), p. A218.

6. Harry Truman, *Memoirs*, Vol. I (Garden City, 1955), p. 501.

7. Sylvester Petro, *The Labor Policy of a Free Society* (New York, 1957), p. 130.

8. As reported in *The New York Times*, January 7, 1947, p. 20.

9. As reported in *The New York Times*, May 18, 1947, p. 1.

10. As reported in *The New York Times*, September 13, 1947, p. 2.

11. Robert A. Taft, "Toward Peace in Labor," *Collier's*, Vol. 121, No. 10 (March 6, 1958), pp. 21 ff.

12. William S. White, *The Taft Story* (New York, 1954), p. 70.

13. Roscoe Pound, "Legal Immunities of Labor Unions," in Chamberlin, Bradley, Reilly, and Pound, *Labor Unions and Public Policy* (Washington, 1958), pp. 149–150.

14. Robert A. Taft, "The Taft-Hartley Act," address to the Philadelphia Bulletin Forum, March 8, 1948; printed in the *Congressional Record*, 80th Congress, 2nd Session, Vol. 94, Part 10 (March 10, 1948), p. A1510.

CHAPTER VII

An Economy Humane and Free

The Charitable Society and the Socialist State

"CREEPING SOCIALISM" and "the welfare state" were terms of anathema with Robert Taft. Not everyone understood what he meant; indeed, some of his Congressional colleagues professed to see in him a doctrinaire of *laissez-faire* in its most rigorous form. Senator Ralph Flanders implied something of that sort when he wrote to Senator Taft, late in 1947, that "I wish the whole party leadership were more positively interested in people."

Taft replied with his habitual directness: "You say that you wish 'the whole party leadership were more positively interested in people.' I feel very strongly that I am interested in people and that the principle which I support will do more good for the people than most of the New Deal ideas of regulation and planned economy. Probably I don't express often enough what my real interest is, because it certainly is not in wealthier people or Big Business or any of those who seem to get some special advantage out of our present system. My belief is that under a free system we are bound to have much greater inequality than under a socialistic system, although in the end I believe the socialistic system would level everybody down rather than up. I believe, however, that we must accept the inequalities and then do our best to improve the condition of the people at the lower end, to a certain extent by economic measures like minimum wage laws, and to a certain extent by direct assistance to health, education, housing and the like."[1]

The free and bountiful American economy, that is, would provide the means for a society charitable in the root meaning of *caritas:* not a Dead-Sea-level socialist egalitarianism, but a system in which the able would realize their practical talents and receive their just rewards, and in which the needy and unfortunate—from out that society's prosperity—would be provided with a tolerable livelihood, regardless of their inability to provide for themselves. Far from being pure Manchesterian dogma, Taft's economic convictions were founded upon Christian moral principles and upon the American historical experience.

The socialist ideology, Taft believed, could not be reconciled with personal liberty—nor with the American democracy; nor would socialism provide adequately, in the long run, for the material wants of man. "Democratic socialism," in Europe and elsewhere, was far gone in decay during Taft's political years, especially after the Second World War; Communism on the Soviet model, indeed, was a real menace, but only because supported by force of arms, systematic subversion, and totalist methods. There existed no prospect that the little Socialist party in America could contrive to master the American political apparatus.

Yet what Taft repeatedly called "creeping socialism" had to be taken seriously. He meant by his term a gradual and half-unconscious increase of bureaucratic direction of the economy, steadily diminishing the rewards of enterprising men, preventing the accumulation of capital, stifling the economy by a fussy paternalism, buying political power by indiscriminate largess of public funds to pressure groups. This veiled and almost mindless socialism would lack both the idealism of the "utopian" socialists, and the grim comparative efficiency of the Soviets; it would amount to national stagnation, and not stagnation of the economy alone. Taft had in mind that "demo-

cratic despotism" so well described by Tocqueville in a famous
passage of *Democracy in America:*

> Above this race of men stands an immense and tutelary
> power, which takes upon itself alone to secure their
> gratifications and to watch over their fate. That power is
> absolute, minute, regular, provident, and mild. It would be
> like the authority of a parent if, like that authority, its
> object was to prepare men for manhood; but it seeks, on
> the contrary, to keep them in perpetual childhood; it is
> well content that the people should rejoice, provided that
> they think of nothing but rejoicing. For their happiness
> such a government willingly labors, but it chooses to be
> the sole agent and the only arbiter of their necessities,
> facilitates their pleasures, manages their principal con-
> cerns, directs their industry, regulates the descent of
> property, and subdivides their inheritances; what remains,
> but to spare them all the care of thinking and all the
> trouble of living?[2]

Taft doubted whether such servitude really would be mild;
but otherwise Tocqueville's prediction fits the "welfare state"
which Taft beheld in twentieth-century Europe. The prospect
of this social enervation and boredom filled Taft with abhorrence, so that he devoted scores of long speeches to sober and
detailed exposition of the corrupting character of such an
ideology and such a social condition.

In opposing the "welfare state," nevertheless, Taft never lost
sight of the promotion of the general welfare which was a
principal object of the federal Constitution. A free economy,
he declared, must best promote the general welfare for the
majority of Americans; yet there remained a comparatively
large minority—usually estimated by Taft as a fifth of the
population—who for one reason or another would not share
tolerably in American prosperity, unless assisted by truly
charitable undertakings, including action by the federal government.

He thought governmental assistance particularly necessary
and hopeful for the rising generation. Children might be

enabled to improve themselves, in time, by practical present improvement of their schooling, their health, and their material environment; not much could be done to rouse adults from apathy or bad habits, even though society should make sure that the improvident and the slack did not suffer privation. When told that such measures of public assistance might diminish the initiative of the needy, he replied that the American poor (always excepting the young) had very little initiative to lose.

Felix Morley, in 1948, competently summarized Taft's position on such social measures:

"It may be news to some, but there are a number of Republican leaders who think that Taft flirts with socialism; that he is 'not quite sound'—meaning thoroughly devoted to the doctrine of *laissez-faire*—in his political and economic theory. There are three counts in this indictment, these being the Senator's sponsorship of those bills favoring federal aid in education, health, and housing. The underlying pattern of these bills is identical. In each case the federal government would be authorized to subsidize state or local authorities anxious to attain certain minimum standards in public education, health, and housing. In each case initiative for improvement is left to the community, and there are careful safeguards against federal usurpation.

"While Senator Taft admits that some aspects of this legislation qualify the principle of free enterprise, he hotly denies that it is necessarily socialistic for the state to come to the aid of individuals who fall behind in the march of life. 'The philosophy of socialism,' he says, 'is to raise all to the average, which necessarily will bring all others down to the same dead level and take all life and progress out of the system. . . . The extreme philosophy the other way is to "let the devil take the hindmost" . . . on the theory that in the end general progress will be faster.'

"Against the philosophy of extreme individualism Senator Taft makes three points. First, it is contrary to the humane instincts of a Christian people, which Americans in general are.

Second, a nation founded on the principle that 'all men are equal' cannot logically permit any of its children to be deprived of opportunity. Third, education, health, and housing are matters which affect the national welfare and therefore justify intervention by the national government."[3]

In an humane economy, Taft repeatedly argued, equality of opportunity—though not equality of final reward—is a matter of public concern, at every level of government. Taft much preferred to have charitable activities conducted by private and voluntary agencies when resources should permit, but he saw that local and state governments must act often—and that the increasing concentration of public revenues in the federal government made it necessary for much assistance to come from the Treasury in Washington. Through grants-in-aid to the several states, hedged about by precautionary clauses which would reserve the administration of such programs to state and local authorities, he hoped to improve the lot of that one-fifth of the nation which was not adequately providing for itself.

Such measures would guard the free economy and the free society against socialism by diminishing the afflictions for which the socialists pretended to offer a radical remedy. "When the Depression of 1929 broke down temporarily the financial foundations on which our economic system was built," he said in 1940, "a lack of confidence naturally arose in the whole system. New conditions had developed to which the American system of political and economic freedom did not sufficiently adjust itself. Conditions had become more complex, but not, I believe, fundamentally different. It was necessary for the Government to assume more social obligations. I feel confident that this could have been done, and can be done today, without changing the spirit or the substance of American life."[4]

The New Dealers, he insisted, offered a cure worse than the disease: their ponderous machine of centralized social control would weaken the economy and injure the character of the people; and in the long run, it would harm those it was meant to assist. As he put it in 1949, "I believe the American people are convinced that with the tremendous productivity of our free country we can prevent extreme hardship and poverty in the U.S. today, that we can maintain a minimum floor under education, health, housing, and food. We have recognized that obligation in the past, but the job has not been systematically done. With Federal aid it can be done, but there are plenty of pitfalls and dangers to liberty in the *way* in which it is done."[5]

These perils were real. The Socialists ignore the importance of incentive, "the fact that most men do not like to work unless there is something to be gained. Lethargy has been the greatest enemy of progress in many sections of the world."[6] Public assistance to the poor should not become assistance to the capable, lest incentive be undone. Nor must the cost of such a program be so vast as to dishearten the productive part of society: that would wring the neck of the goose laying the golden eggs. He put this point well in the last months of his life:

"Big Government has constantly increased in size and power. Twenty years ago the Federal Government took 6 per cent of the people's income. Today they are spending 28 per cent of the people's income and the taxes run over 25 per cent. When we add to that about 7 or 8 per cent for State and local government, we find that the total tax burden today is approximately 30 per cent of the people's income and Government spending more than a third of that national income. This means that the Federal Government is conducting over 28 per cent of the total activity of the people of this country and other governments 7 or 8 per cent. Frankly, I do not believe that we can impose on the people a burden of total government in excess of about 25 per cent of the people's income, if we really desire to continue a free economy. The taxation required becomes exceedingly burdensome, so burdensome that it is almost impossible to balance the budget, and creates an inflation which destroys the whole basis of the system on which a free economy and rewards and incentives are based. . . . At some point this burden becomes so great that there is a constant spiral of further government activity and we find it just as easy to socialize a country through the expenditure of money as by direct taking-over of industry."[7]

How might the American government and the American economy provide a decent minimum standard of living for every family, a satisfactory educational opportunity for everyone, and tolerable medical attention for the whole population, without disheartening measures of socialism? Taft asked and answered those questions repeatedly, and his approach was that of a practical statesman, earnestly concerned for the general welfare. He did not hesitate to recommend action by the federal government; but it must be prudent action, controlled by checks upon central power and awareness of the need for frugality.

"Nor do we adopt any *laissez-faire* principle," he said in 1950. "Federal action is often essential to maintain liberty itself in industry by preventing monopoly and unfair competition. Federal action can prevent economic oppression by setting a standard for a minimum wage. It can prevent economic inequality by some reasonable price-support program to prevent the destruction of agricultural purchasing power through forces far beyond the control of the individual or the united farmers.

"Every proposal for Federal action, however, must be judged by its effect on the liberty of the individual, the family, the community, industry, and labor. Such liberty cannot be sacrificed to any theoretical improvement from Government control or Governmental spending."[8]

The general safeguards which he specified were four: first, "the total expense must not be unfair to the four-fifths who pay the bill"; second, local and state authorities must administer the measures; third, "the standards on which aid is granted should be clearly stated in the Federal statute"; fourth, this aid should be confined to the "lower-income groups."[9] These principles are better understood by turning to three positive programs for national social improvement which Taft offered:

aid to schools, aid for the betterment of health, and aid for public housing.

Equality of Opportunity in Education

Throughout his first five years in the Senate, Taft stoutly opposed all bills designed to grant federal subsidies to public schools. Almost unaided, he defeated the proposal of Senators Thomas and Hill, in 1943, to appropriate three hundred million dollars for this purpose.

It was not that Taft believed such programs to be unconstitutional; on the contrary, education had been "socialized" for a hundred years, he remarked, and there existed ample precedent for limited federal grants-in-aid in this field. His objections, instead, were concerned with the danger of control of schooling from Washington, in an age of ideology; with the possibility that such appropriations might become political plums, given the centralizing tendency of the New Deal; with the financial difficulty of finding the money during the Second World War; and with the question of necessity.

After 1943, nevertheless, gradually he became the most effective proponent of such subsidies—although Congress declined to pass any general bill of that sort during his lifetime. Circumstances had altered, he perceived. For during the Second World War, public schools, like housing, had been neglected, and immense sums of money must be found somewhere to repair that neglect and to provide for the swelling school-population.[10] Most states still could supply their own educational necessities; yet those with relatively small revenues —particularly some eleven Southern states—were urgently in need of assistance.

Besides, public instruction was a matter of national concern, he argued, though not a matter for central direction; and ignorance and lack of opportunity in some states would affect all states. His general principle was expressed in an address to the American Council on Education, in 1949. The federal government, he said, should confine itself to seeing that a decent minimum was provided for the schooling of children in states where a need of assistance clearly existed:

"I feel very strongly that in the educational field—as in health, in welfare, and in housing—the primary responsibility and right belong to the state and local governments. This is our constitutional system. I do not know whether the federal government has power actually to regulate those fields. It has power to spend money in them, which is derived from the spending power, the power to levy taxes for the general welfare; but there is no direct mention of power in the welfare field or in the field of education in the federal Constitution. I think the federal function is a secondary one in education, to come along and see that it is possible for the state to do its job. The necessity for it arises very largely out of the limited tax power of the state. The state cannot reach the most lucrative sources of taxation because it has competition from other states. If a higher income tax is imposed in a state, people will move to the next state, or they will move to Florida where they do not have an income tax."[11]

Taft's plan for assistance to public schools is best seen in his bill of 1948—which was passed by the Senate, but was rejected by the House. By its terms, three hundred million dollars would have been appropriated for educational aid to states, in proportion to need. The poorest states would have received about $28.50 per child enrolled in public schools; the most prosperous, a minimum of $5 per child. Quantitatively, North Carolina, Alabama, and Texas would have been the most conspicuous beneficiaries; Taft's own state of Ohio would have gained very little fiscally, and Taft himself would have gained nothing politically from this proposal.

Administration of the plan would have been left entirely to the states, to avert any possibility of federal interference with state and local powers—with what Orestes Brownson had called "territorial democracy." Whether state governments might extend this aid to private and parochial schools was left to the policies of the several states, as was the question of whether aid should be allocated to schools racially segregated.*

Despite these painstaking guarantees of freedom from federal control of educational policy, Congress declined to act. The reasons for congressional reluctance were several: first, the dispute over whether aid should be permitted or forbidden for church-connected schools, in which quarrel Congressmen found themselves between the Scylla of Catholic political power and the Charybdis of the National Education Association; second, the unwillingness of the more prosperous states to submit to general taxation for the benefit of the poorer states; third, the fear that once the flood-gates of federal assistance to schools should be opened, the federal budget might be drained insufferably by state and local demands (reinforced by the school administrators' and teachers' lobby) for increasing help, in an activity formerly financed almost

---

* Taft said that he had employed, in his bill, the strongest possible language to prevent interference with public educational policies by officials of the federal government. Section 2 of the bill read as follows:

> Nothing contained in this act shall be construed to authorize any department, agency, officer, or employee of the United States to exercise any direction, supervision, or control over, or to prescribe any requirements with respect to any school, or any State educational institution or agency, with respect to which any funds have been or may be made available or expended pursuant to this act, nor shall any term or condition of any agreement or any other action taken under this act, whether by agreement or otherwise, relating to any contribution made under this act to or on behalf of any school, or any State educational institution or agency, or any limitation or provision in any appropriation made pursuant to this act, seek to control in any manner, or prescribe requirements with respect to, or authorize any department, agency, officer, or employee of the United States to direct, supervise, or control in any manner, or prescribe any requirements with respect to, the administration, the personnel, the curriculum, the instruction, the methods of instruction, or the materials of instruction, nor shall any provision of this act be interpreted or construed to imply or require any change in any State constitution prerequisite to any State sharing the benefits of this act.

(See remarks of Senator Taft, *Congressional Record,* 80th Congress, 2nd Session, 1948, Vol. XCIV, Part 3, p. 3347.)

wholly by state and local revenues. Even the authority and influence of Taft were insufficient to overcome these misgivings; and the proposals of the Truman, Eisenhower, and Kennedy administrations were rejected by Congress, often by burying the bills in House committees or conference committees.

Not until President Johnson's overwhelming victory in the elections of 1964 was it possible for a national administration to push through Congress a bill for massive aid to public schools. The federal-aid measures adopted in 1965 were contrary to the principles recommended by Taft in the 'forties, however. The largess was general, rather than founded upon pressing need in the poorer states: indeed, prosperous school districts profited more than poor ones, because of a principle of matching funds and because of the difficulty experienced by schools with a small staff in dealing with the complexities of the act. Direct aid was not allowed to parochial schools— which, nevertheless, were thrown a bone in the form of the "fringe benefits" of free textbooks and other minor features. Federal control of educational policy promptly was asserted by officials of the Department of Health, Education, and Welfare—and with difficulty was rebuffed, for the moment, by the city of Chicago and other districts that had not anticipated interference with local policy in the North, at least.

In fine, Taft's charitable policy of assistance to those states in pressing need, founded upon a concept of national interest, and confined by strict guarantees of state and local autonomy in policy, never has been enacted. The "equalization fund" advocated by Taft remains unachieved.

The Nation's Health and Socialized Medicine

Socialized medicine would be a curse; but prudent governmental assistance to improve the health of people of low income is a national benefit, Robert Taft reasoned. During his time in the Senate, the Beveridge Plan was adopted in Britain, and the British National Health Service came into being. He desired nothing of that sort for the United States. Yet he earnestly supported programs calculated to provide reasonable medical services for those elements of the population long neglected.

Taft entered into this discussion during 1939 and 1940, when Senator Wagner's Health Bill came before Congress. To provide medical aid for the needy, through one system or another, was sound public policy, Taft said; but the New Dealers meant, in effect, to socialize the medical profession and to establish a centralized medical service that would be inferior to the unregulated services already in existence.

There was nothing revolutionary about governmental activity in this realm, Taft declared: "Every state in the Union has considered that field as a proper one for Government activity. Public health work, particularly in the prevention of communicable disease, has been undertaken without question or doubt. In the field of hospitalization nearly all the states and many cities have provided free general hospitals, and other hospitals for the mentally ill, the tubercular, the epileptics, and other special groups. In connection with general hospitals, local governments have long provided free medical care in greater or less degree."[12] Private charities and the medical profession itself had done generous work on an impressive scale.

What with the phenomenal improvement of public health and medical science in recent years, Taft continued, the New Dealers' advocacy of grandiose federal intervention in this public concern was afflicted by gross exaggeration of the need. Nevertheless, measures should be taken to provide for the sudden costs of catastrophic illness and for other contingencies. The best plan, he thought, was voluntary medical insurance—financed in part, when necessary, by state and federal subsidies. Compulsory insurance he vehemently opposed:

"Deductions from payroll or otherwise to support compulsory health insurance really destroy the whole character of the plan as insurance. Such payments are in fact taxes, and they are shortly absorbed in costs and passed on as taxes to all the people. The assistance which is received comes finally from a Government bureau. Look at the payroll taxes we already have for unemployment insurance, so heavy and complicated in administration as to hamper and restrict the development of private industry and increase unemployment. Health insurance should certainly be developed on a voluntary basis."[13]

Volition must be preserved, too, in the individual's choice of a physician, and in the whole medical profession. "The socialization of the medical profession is a danger which must and can be avoided in any extension of medical aid to the needy. If that aid is confined to the needy the danger is not so great, but even then methods can certainly be developed to give the man entitled to Government aid the right to choose his own doctor and have him paid by the Government. . . .

"But if the Government undertakes to cover the whole field and extend aid not only to the needy, but also to those quite able to pay for it, there is real danger. Compulsory health insurance for all employees, similar to unemployment insurance, would gradually result in a large proportion of the total payments to doctors coming out of the Government fund. In effect, the bulk of the medical profession would be employed by the Federal Government. This is socialization of medicine. We might try to guard against it by provisions allowing the patient to choose his own doctor, but it is not likely that we could long maintain such a restriction."[14]

That scheme would degrade doctors into a servile condition —to which no profession in America had yet been reduced; and a medical dole, indiscriminately applied, would degrade the character of its recipients. The problem was one of relief of those genuinely in need, and the improvement of such conditions only would be made more difficult by adoption of a scheme providing benefits for those quite able to meet their own medical costs. Still, state and local governments had begun to experience trouble in finding the money to improve public health. Taft was willing to commence a program of federal subsidies, if a sound one could be drawn up; but that program should be merely auxiliary, administration remaining in the hands of the state governments. The Wagner Bill, typical of the New Deal, would impose an immense bureaucratic apparatus, a crushing burden upon the Treasury and upon the medical profession, when the true need was for particular programs consonant with the American political structure.

Taft outlined alternative approaches. He recommended federal grants to assist the states in building small hospitals in rural areas—which, incidentally, would encourage the states to study all their problems in public health. More, he believed that Congress should begin to study plans for subsidies to direct medical aid for the needy. "We owe a duty to the unfortunate members of society who, without fault of their own, or even perhaps with fault of their own, are unable to provide a decent living for their families. We owe the children of such families an equal opportunity to make a success of their lives. They cannot do so in a family overwhelmed by poverty and illness. No system will work to relieve all hardship. No system will be 100 per cent perfect. But I believe that at a reasonable cost the Federal Government can stimulate interest and assist the development of plans that will reduce the hardships of many unfortunate families. . . . But let's do it the right way. . . . Let's not do it in a way which will only give the needy the kind of treatment a poor citizen gets from a Government bureaucrat in Washington."[15]

Taft consistently adhered to these opinions of 1940. In 1945 and 1946, he supported—and helped to pass—the Hill-Burton Bill, providing for federal matching grants-in-aid to encourage the construction of hospitals by states, local governments, and voluntary organizations.

In 1947, he campaigned against the Wagner-Murray-Dingell Bill for compulsory health insurance, "not only a socialization of medicine, but . . . the federalization of medicine."[16] As an alternative to this proposal for state medicine, he—together with Senators Ball and Smith—introduced a different bill, generally called the Taft Health Bill. Taft's measure (National Health Bill S.

545) provided that there should be created a National Health Agency, consolidating all federal services of this character; and that federal subsidies be appropriated to assist states in providing general health, medical, and hospital services to individuals and families of low income. A National Institute of Dental Research would be established, and grants-in-aid made for the study and prevention of cancer. The subsidies to state governments would amount to two hundred million dollars, initially, proportioned according to need and population, on the basis of matching appropriations by the participating states; states would be authorized to set up "voluntary prepayment health plans" (subsidized medical insurance, through contract with private insurance companies).

Neither the welfare-state measure called the Wagner-Murray-Dingell Bill, nor the Taft Health Bill to improve the health of the poor through matching grants to states, was approved by Congress. Out of the debate, nevertheless, there emerged—with Senator Taft's support—the National Dental Research Act and the National Heart Act.

In 1948, President Truman, in his "Omnibus Bill," endeavored to revive the scheme of compulsory health insurance. Taft successfully opposed the plan, which, he said, was not insurance at all, "but the providing of free medical care to all the people of the United States," and which would have cost four or five billion dollars a year. Together with other Truman recommendations, and with existing old-age and un-employment systems, this undertaking would have required a deduction from payrolls of eighteen per cent—disguised and insufferably heavy taxation.

That portion of the "Omnibus Bill" was defeated. Meanwhile, Taft co-sponsored a bill to provide thirty-five million dollars for state health programs for school children—which did not emerge from the House of Representatives. With Senators Hill, Ellender, and Smith, Taft did succeed in improving the Hill-Burton Act of 1946, extending and increasing grants to states for the construction of hospitals.

As he had explained in 1947, Taft's object in working for federal subsidies for public health was not equality of condition, but rather the relief of positive need. "In deploring the relative condition of the least fortunate 20 per cent of our population," he had written in *Collier's*, "we should not forget the healthy condition of the other four-fifths, and the opportunities for improvement our system offers to all. We must try to eliminate the poverty, ignorance, illness and hardships of the 20 per cent, and brighten their opportunities, but there is no sense in trying to solve their distressing problems by pulling down the living level of the normal four-fifths. It's stupid to level the majority downward in order to narrow the gap between it and the minority. Let's lift the minority. . . . In general I have not been opposed to the extension of governmental activity as such. I do not see, for example, that extension of governmental activity in the field of social welfare, if properly limited and administered, can interfere with freedom. In many cases it is necessary to assure freedom and opportunity to families who do not otherwise have it."[17]

The all-embracing and compulsory systems of medical assistance which Taft heartily disliked did not find favor with Congress until twelve years after his death. Then the Medicare act of 1965 provided medical attention—though limited in scope for the individual—for everyone over sixty-five years of age. Presumably this plan would have aroused Taft's opposition. It was compulsory; it began at the wrong end of the scale (for Taft was concerned principally with the needs of the young, while the elderly have larger savings than any other category of the population); it did not discriminate between those able to pay their own expenses and those really in need of assistance; it was founded upon a general tax through the Social Security system, borne almost equally by the affluent and the poor; it did not provide for catastrophic or really prolonged sickness. As a general largess, Medicare was calculated to win votes for a political party; yet it was not truly addressed to that help for the needy which Taft had endeavored to develop.

Federal Aid in Housing

Although Robert Taft's concern with low-cost, publicly subsidized housing for those in need may be traced back to his early years in the Senate, Taft did not enter upon leadership in this field until he was appointed chairman of the Senate subcommittee on housing and urban redevelopment, in 1943. A whole volume could be written about his work for public housing thereafter. As Lee F. Johnson, executive vice-president of the National Housing Conference, wrote a few months after Taft's death, "Low-income families of this country may never fully realize the strength that Senator Taft's consistent advocacy of decent homes for all American families meant to their cause. It took years of study for him to develop the housing principles that he so ably espoused and defended."[18]

Neglect and lack of permanent construction during the Second World War had taken a severe toll of American housing; for that matter, the relative cessation of building during the Great Depression had not been compensated for by 1943. Temporary housing built during those years already was decaying. It is clear that several million people, at least, experienced real difficulty in finding any lodging at a price or rent commensurate with their incomes.

During his study of the difficulty, Senator Taft rejected the theory that if sufficient expensive new housing should be built, older dwellings would become available for people of low income. He rejected, too, a proposal for a type of federally-subsidized rent certificate, to be issued to poor families, saying that it would not suffice.* And he became convinced

* A close student of Taft's housing proposals, Charles Brown, points out that Taft did not oppose on principle all rent-certificate plans: "The type of rent certificate Taft opposed, as put forward in the

that only the erection of new housing in the cities, made possible by federal grants-in-aid, could provide a satisfactory remedy.

This low-cost public housing must not be luxurious, for funds were limited; and it would destroy incentives to self-help among working people if housing for the needy were superior to the accommodation of Americans above the subsistence level. Quarters in these housing projects should be available only to applicants whose incomes were inadequate to provide for their renting tolerable housing at local costs.

It might be tedious to attempt to trace in detail Taft's intricate struggle, as *de facto* leader of the minority party, to restrain the liberal Democrats from embarking upon elaborately costly and impractical schemes of housing, and to tug after himself those Republican conservatives in whose eyes any form of public housing was suspect. He was accused of having turned socialist—though his purpose was a conservative end, the restoration of a satisfactory existence for the uprooted and impoverished. President Truman and Senator Taft were at loggerheads; yet in the end their rival plans for housing were joined in an act which could not have been passed without Taft's support.

Taft's housing bill of 1945—of which Senators Wagner and Ellender were co-sponsors—was based on the estimate that some 1,250,000 housing units must be built every year for the

---

Truman years, would have put more money in the pockets of landlords without requiring them to improve the condition of the housing they rented to low-income groups. While he thought public housing the best solution he could discover as a means of providing decent shelter for the very poor, opposed the above-mentioned type of rent certificate, and regarded subsidization of commercially built low-rent housing as impractical because few commercial builders were likely to be interested in it, Taft did not oppose rent certificates for persons living in non-profit housing developments for poverty-stricken families."

Taft did suggest that charitable organizations might be induced by federal subsidies to build housing and make it available at rents below the cost of amortization and maintenance—a proposal resembling the "rent supplements" program of the Johnson administration, advanced in 1965.

next ten years, if the population of America were to be decently lodged; and of this number, about two-thirds must be intended for people who could not afford to pay more than forty dollars a month in rent. Taft proposed that ten per cent of the annual construction of housing—that is, 125,000 units per year—should be governmentally subsidized low-rent housing; the remaining nine-tenths, or 1,125,000 units per year, would be private, unsubsidized construction. (Purchase of the private housing would be made easier by an increase of funds for the Federal Home Loan Bank and the Federal Housing Administration, lending money at low interest rates, and by government-guaranteed home loans to veterans.) The subsidized housing would be provided only on the request of city councils, and would be available only for people with incomes at least twenty per cent below the level estimated, in a particular city, as adequate rental for decent housing.

Taft's bill was appoved by the Senate in April, 1946, but was rejected by the House; nor was he able to obtain passage of it in 1947. Taft told his colleagues, in 1947, that the federal government now could afford to spend a billion dollars a year for housing, public health, education, and other measures of public welfare; the need for housing was especially acute, for the 1940 housing census had shown that of twenty-nine million American dwelling units, six million were substandard, unfit for the rearing of children. Yet Taft's proposals were rejected a third time in the second session of the Eightieth Congress, 1948, strong though his influence was at that time.

Undiscouraged, Taft carried his case to the public. Of his many speeches on this subject, one of the ablest was an address in New York early in 1949. He exposed several fallacies in the controversy over public housing, and went on to defend subsidized projects—which, he pointed out, would not be competitive with private building, since the tenants of the public projects could not possibly afford to rent or buy even the cheapest new private housing.

"Public housing is criticized as being too expensive," he said. "It does seem to me that the limits in the Ellender bill which would permit the expenditure of about $12,500 per housing unit are very high indeed. Four room homes can be built for $7,500, perhaps $6,500. Some public housing projects perhaps have to be fire proof and involve greater expense. But if this program is to avoid public criticism, it must be carried out in most places at far below the Ellender bill limits. We ought not to give a man who is admittedly unable to earn anything like an average wage better housing than the man who works hard and builds his own home."

The erection of decent public housing in blighted areas would tend to revive private activity and building in the city cores. "My belief is that if we take the edge off the problem at the bottom, destroy many of the existing slums and set an example in many neighborhoods, it will not be necessary to extend the public housing program beyond a total of perhaps a million homes in the course of the next ten years. I have seen public housing projects in Cleveland, and elsewhere, which have changed the whole character of the neighborhood. Private owners have come in and improved all the homes in the neighboring section, new stores have been built and a standard established extending far beyond the number of homes covered by public housing."

Private industry alone could not possibly provide for this especial need, he concluded. If men of business and owners of property unintelligently should oppose federal subsidies without offering any alternative for the poor, they only would be inviting more radical measures and furnishing with ammunition the hostile critics of the American free economy. He appealed for understanding:

"I have found no alternative to public housing as a method of providing low income rentals to those at the bottom of the income scale. Public housing is still experimental and the experiment has been very much confused by the intervening of the Second World War and the large amount of war housing constructed directly or indirectly by the government. Many of the complaints against the public housing system relate to this war housing. Few cities have been able to give the public housing program a proper trial, and many cities require the urban redevelopment assistance provided in the Ellender bill in order to handle the slum question properly."[19]

The more well-housed and contented families there are, Taft remarked on several occasions, the more enduring will be the American political structure. And the building of these projects, which without grants-in-aid would not be constructed at all, would stimulate the economy as military production fell off. Control of the program should be in the hands of state and local authorities, and the federal government should offer assistance only after local initiative had been manifested. Gradually Taft, by these earnest arguments, brought around to his views sufficient Republicans to make a big housing act thinkable.

Meanwhile, President Truman had been at work designing a mammoth housing bill, as a part of the "Fair Deal" (the only major feature of the Fair Deal, indeed, which was to obtain enactment). The Truman plan incorporated much that Taft had been struggling for, but went far beyond Taft's in its scale and cost. Though Truman had denounced Taft as the cold-hearted representative of selfish interests, he had, in effect, stolen the Republican's clothes while Taft was campaigning for public housing.

In its concluding months, the Eightieth Congress had passed a housing bill that incorporated some features of the Taft-Ellender-Wagner Bill; Taft had called this act inadequate, but had voted for it; and Truman had condemned it as parsimonious, but had signed it. After his victory in the elections of 1948, Truman was ready to advance his administration bill for subsidized housing.

So the Democratic Eighty-first Congress passed a bill far more expensive than the one Taft had drafted. The Housing Act of 1949 authorized, among many other provisions, the construction of 810,000 low-income housing units. Taft's support for this measure, whatever his reservations, brought about its enactment; indeed, much of it was the culmination of his work over the preceding six years. Without Taft's help, there would have been no such act. Richard O. Davies summarizes Taft's contribution to this reform:

"He gave the legislation the necessary bipartisan support to enable it to pass the Senate; about twenty Republicans followed his leadership on housing. Without these votes the bill would never have become law. Taft also gave the bill the endorsement of responsible conservatism; frequently, liberals cited Taft as an example of an enlightened conservative who saw public housing in its correct perspective. Finally, Taft served as a brake upon more avid public housing enthusiasts, who preferred a far more expansive program, which probably would have alienated many moderates who supported the bill."[20]

Despite Taft's labor to define the objects of public housing and to make systematic all federal projects of this character, no mind comparable to Taft's has analyzed or controlled this field since Taft's death. It is somewhat discouraging to learn that of all the funds spent upon "urban renewal" in recent years, only five per cent have been utilized for the rehousing of the crowds displaced by demolition of old buildings. Taft thought a great deal about the people who could not afford to pay prevailing rents; accusations that Taft was "unsympathetic to the common man" fall far from the mark. For Taft, urban renewal was not primarily a commercial undertaking, but a work of duty on behalf of the unfortunate. Some of the social reforms he recommended would lie dormant until President Johnson's "war on poverty"—and then would appear in a form less practical and less coherent than Taft had designed.

The Credo of an Humane Politician

A humane commonwealth in which a free economy would make possible the steady improvement of the lot of an economically depressed one-fifth of the population, without recourse to the totalist devices of socialism: this was Robert Taft's design. He was, after all, "interested in people"—and more sincerely and effectually interested in the relief of want than were many of the vociferous and attitudinizing radical champions of humanitarian reform.

From time to time, during his years in national politics, Taft issued a press release or leaflet called "My Political Credo," varying somewhat in content with the controversies of the year. The "Credo" distributed about 1950 is a good summary of his views on social improvement—particularly its sections entitled "Promote a Higher Standard of Living" and "Equality of Opportunity."

"Obviously, a higher standard of living depends on the operation at full speed of our economic machine," Taft wrote. "Experience has shown that it runs more freely under private control than under the deadening hand of government. I believe very strongly that progress can only be made through private initiative and through incentive to people to work hard.

"A higher standard of living is not produced by government handouts. It is not produced by government regulation or government operation. A higher standard of living depends upon a free economy and the machine which it creates. But the very nature of a free economy means inequality in the economic standing of different individuals. It cannot give men any return to which their abilities and efforts do not entitle them."

This competitive economy, nevertheless, would provide the foundation for communal generosity, including subsidies from the federal treasury for those unable to make their own way; and thus equality of opportunity would be made possible:

"To eliminate hardship and poverty and even more to assure equality of opportunity for the children of those who do not receive sufficient income, I believe that a floor under family requirements is necessary.

"There can be no equality of opportunity if the child does not have at least a primary school education, adequate medical care, sufficient food and clothing and decent shelter. A few may rise above the handicaps of poverty, but the great majority are condemned to an inadequate, perhaps unhappy life.

"We have long provided free education. We have provided much free medical care, but there are gaps, particularly in the poorer states and rural sections. We have done least in the housing field and in the elimination of slums.

"I favor federal action in these fields because the state resources are, in many respects and in many places, inadequate. And the states do not have the sources of taxation open to the federal government.

"But we must recognize, first, that aid of this kind to give men something which they do not earn through their own abilities can only be paid by taxing the productive workers. That taxation cannot be too heavy or it will destroy the very incentive whch keeps the machine operating at high speed.

"A floor under these services, therefore, cannot be too high. Furthermore, financial aid is likely to destroy the incentive of those other than the children who receive the assistance. Certainly, the government must not destroy the incentive of other workers by providing a higher standard for non-workers than for those who earn their own way.

"I am very much opposed to a government program which will attempt to provide free medical care for all people, free housing for all, or free subsistence. That indeed would be socialism. That would destroy the very machinery which makes it possible—perhaps for the first time in the world—to eliminate hardship and poverty and give equal opportunity to every child.

"With this framework we must adopt an affirmative program to secure liberty, justice, and equality of opportunity. We must seek an improvement in standards of material well-being within the principles of liberty, justice and equality. That is the way to a better life in America. That is the way to progress and production. That is the way to safety and peace. That is the way to a people strong, self-reliant and happy."

These were the words of conviction, not of time-serving. "I

believe there is one great issue in the world today," Taft concluded. "It is that of government operated by a free people on the basis of freedom and justice for every individual, on the one hand, against the totalitarian state on the other—the kind of state which concentrates in a central government power to direct the lives of all its people, its agriculture, its commerce and its industry."[21]

Robert Taft had been no leveler, and he had aspired to something better than the mass society of *Brave New World* or *1984*. For him, the "general welfare" did not mean the welfare rolls; and the measures of reform which he designed were intended to make the "welfare state" an anachronism.

Notes, CHAPTER VII

1.   Ralph Flanders to Robert Taft, November 24, 1947; Robert Taft to Ralph Flanders, November 27, 1947. Robert A. Taft Papers, Library of Congress.

2.   Alexis de Tocqueville, *Democracy in America* (edited by Phillips Bradley, New York, 1948), Vol. II, p. 318.

3.   Felix Morley, "The Case for Taft," *Life*, Vol. 24, No. 6 (February 9, 1948), pp. 51, 55.

4.   Robert A. Taft, "Printing and Its Contribution to Democracy," speech before the Baltimore Association of Commerce and the Graphic Arts Association of Baltimore, February 27, 1940; printed in the *Congressional Record*, 76th Congress, 3rd Session, Vol. 86, Part 14 (March 6, 1940), p. A1226.

5.   Robert A. Taft, "The Republican Party," *Fortune*, Vol. XXXIX, No. 4 (April, 1949), p. 112.

6.   *Ibid.*, p. 110.

7.   Robert A. Taft, "Freedom: the Key to Progress," speech before the National Canners' Association, Chicago, February 21,

1953; printed in the *Congressional Record*, 83rd Congress, 1st Session, Vol. 99, Part 9 (February 25, 1953), p. A877.

8. Robert A. Taft, speech to the Maine Republican Convention, at Portland, Maine, March 31, 1950; printed in the *Congressional Record*, 81st Congress, 2nd Session, Vol. 96, Part 14 (April 4, 1950), p. A2532.

9. Robert A. Taft, "A Republican Program for Progress," speech delivered at Columbus, Ohio, to the Ohio Federation of Republican Women's Organizations, October 19, 1945; printed in the *Congressional Record*, 79th Congress, 1st Session, Vol. 91, Part 13 (October 22, 1945), p. A4425.

10. On this point, see Roger Freeman, *Financing the Public Schools:* Vol. I, *School Needs in the Decade Ahead* (Washington, 1958), particularly Chapter VI, "Classrooms."

11. Robert A. Taft, "Education in the Congress," address to the annual meeting of the American Council on Education, at Washington, D.C., May 9, 1949; printed in *The Educational Record*, Vol. 30, No. 3 (July 1949), p. 346.

12. Robert A. Taft, "Medical Aid for the Needy," speech before the Ohio State Medical Association, at Cincinnati, Ohio, May 16, 1940; printed in the *Congressional Record*, 76th Congress, 3rd Session, Vol. 86, Part 15 (May 21, 1940), p. A3105.

13. *Ibid.*, p. A3106.

14. *Ibid.*

15. *Ibid.*, p. A3107.

16. Robert A. Taft, "A Republican Program," radio address, January 3, 1947; printed in the *Congressional Record*, 80th Congress, 1st Session, Vol. 93, Part 10 (January 6, 1947), p. A8.

17. Robert A. Taft, "No Substitute for Freedom," *Collier's*, Vol. 119, No. 5 (February 1, 1947), p. 13.

18. Lee F. Johnson, "Bob Taft—Champion of Low-Rent Public Housing," *Catholic Charities Review*, Vol. 37 (September 1953), p. 173.

19. Robert A. Taft, "Private Enterprise Has Not Solved Housing Problem," address to the Graduate School of Business Administration of New York University and the Mortgage Bankers Association of America; printed in *The Commercial and Financial Chronicle*, Vol. 169, No. 4774 (February 3, 1949), pp. 15, 30, 31.

20. Richard O. Davies, " 'Mr. Republican' Turns 'Socialist': Robert A. Taft and Public Housing," *Ohio History*, Vol. 75, No. 3 (Summer 1964), p. 143.

21. Robert A. Taft, "My Political Credo," c. 1950. Copy in Robert A. Taft Papers, Library of Congress.

CHAPTER VIII

A Foreign Policy for Americans

An Isolationist?

NOT EVEN Robert Taft's labor legislation provoked so much hostility from liberals and radicals as did his endeavor to present a conservative foreign policy, in opposition to the diplomatic and military measures of the Roosevelt and Truman administrations. A dozen years ago, the current of opinion among serious journalists and professors of politics ran strongly against Taft's view of the American interest in international concerns. His biographer William S. White, for instance, wrote that Taft's final speech on foreign policy (read to the National Conference of Christians and Jews, meeting in Cincinnati in May 1953, by Robert Taft, Jr., as his father lay in a Cincinnati hospital) constituted "the last inconsistency of a hundred inconsistencies, though this time a genial one, of a man whose record in world affairs was inconsistent almost to the point of inconceivability."[1]

Some inconsistencies indeed may be discerned in Taft's positions in international affairs. Yet if one examines the decisions and speeches of Roosevelt, Truman, Vandenberg, Acheson, Hull, or any other political leader more steadily concerned with diplomacy and war, during those years, than was Taft, one encounters at least an equal degree of "inconsistency." It could not have been otherwise.

For the diplomacy of a great power cannot be conducted with a rigorous consistency, on doctrines enunciated at some fixed moment in the past, without regard for altered circumstances. International statecraft, even more than domestic politics, is the art of the possible; today any political leader who should attempt to base decisions in foreign policy solely upon some manual or crib drawn up decades earlier would be a wretched failure—and a danger to his country. In diplomacy, a foolish consistency really is the hobgoblin of little minds. In the affairs of nations, circumstances alter with giddy rapidity: the Soviet Russia of 1953, for instance, was not quite the Soviet Russia of 1939, in strength or in aspiration. If Taft—or Roosevelt, or Truman—had advocated inflexible consistency, immutable adherence to his opinions on foreign policy in 1938, say—regardless of changes in the world occurring during the Second World War—he would have been a remarkably stupid man. Respect for general principles in the conduct of diplomacy is one thing; dogmatic fidelity to one's own opinions under different conditions years earlier, quite another thing. And prudence, not "consistency," is the principal virtue in a statesman.[2]

That Robert Taft changed his mind on some aspects of American foreign policy, and from time to time was ambiguous on other points, did not distinguish him from other men of his generation concerned with diplomacy and war. Within Taft's own party, the inconsistencies and ambiguities of Arthur Vandenberg—not to mention Wendell Willkie—were more conspicuous than Taft's: Vandenberg shifted abruptly from the most marked "isolationism" to the most accommodating internationalism. To demand from Taft, who never possessed executive power, a consistency superior to that of other political leaders, and independent of the changing world and of experience's lessons, is to ask what statecraft cannot afford.

Consistent or not, Robert Taft's attack on the foreign policies of the Roosevelt and Truman administrations usually was popular. A critic hostile toward Taft's concept of foreign policy, Professor John P. Armstrong, concedes that Taft spoke for American popular opinion:

"It must be said that as far as his opinions on foreign policy were concerned, Senator Taft was more than Mr. Republican. He was Mr. American. It was he, perhaps better than anyone else, who voiced the doubts and prejudices, the hopes and fears, the frustrations, the hesitations, and the dissatisfactions that the American people felt as they slowly and ponderously went about the business of adjusting to their changed role in the world. . . . From the Neutrality Act to the truce in Korea he expressed most eloquently—and often with precisely the correct note of petulance—the protest of the American people. Moreover, Senator Taft performed two important services in the field of foreign policy. By his opposition he caused thoughtful Americans constantly to rethink their position, if only to refute him, and he repeatedly reminded the country that there *are* limitations on what we as a nation can and should do in the field of foreign affairs. Those limitations were not as great as Senator Taft, with his consistent lack of imagination as to the potentialities of democratic capitalism, would have us believe. But he acted as a brake upon the wild plans of the emotional humanitarians, on the one hand, and the utopians with their variety of nostrums on the other."[3]

Still, Armstrong concludes, Taft had no foreign policy—merely prejudices and attitudes toward foreign affairs. Such criticism of Taft on international concerns, common enough in popular magazines and in scholarly journals all during his senatorial years, ignores the fact that Robert Taft did possess a general principle for the conduct of foreign relations—and consistently maintained that principle, though necessarily varying its application according to circumstance.

That principle was not peculiar to Taft, nor to the Republican party. It was the postulate upon which every successful foreign policy has been conducted by those chiefs of state or foreign ministers whom historians recognize as adept in diplomacy. In the American experience, it was employed by John Adams, John Quincy Adams, Daniel Webster, Theodore

Roosevelt, and the other able architects of America's foreign policies. It is the principle best described in our time by Professor Hans Morganthau; and it is called the principle of the national interest.

For the object of American foreign policy, Taft argued repeatedly, is to protect and advance American national interests. Neutrality or intervention, alliances and restrictions upon armaments, international commercial agreements and assistance to other governments, peace or war, all must be determined by reference to the effects of such policies upon the security and the welfare of the United States of America. This principle abandoned, any government must be all at sea in its conduct of relations with other powers. The statesman not concerned primarily with the national interest is tossed about by every wind of doctrine; he pursues with imprudent passion vague ideological objectives, and soon finds himself mired in diplomatic and military quicksands.

In international affairs, Taft declared, the New Dealers forever tilted, like so many Quixotes, against windmills. Their objects never well defined even in their own minds, they talked of perpetual peace and the "Four Freedoms"; they dreamed of a universal democratic order on the American model; they conjured up stereotypes of nations, and sought to make alliances with—or wars upon—those deceptive simulacra. Meanwhile, the principle of America's national interest went glimmering. And while utopian fantasies occupied the imagination of the men responsible for American foreign policy, the other powers of the world—states allied or states hostile—continued to act, to their advantage and to America's loss, upon the ineluctable principle of *their* national interests. Britain, Germany, France, Japan, and even Soviet Russia (despite the Soviet pretense of international objectives purely ideological) conducted their diplomacy in a fashion calculated to secure, first of all, old-fangled national advantage; only American political leaders sincerely entertained the fallacy that foreign policy is a facile instrument of "moral righteousness," or that it somehow may open the doors to the Terrestrial Paradise.

Robert Taft may have been correct, or he may have been erroneous, on different occasions, in his understanding of where American national interest lay; but he did not lack a first principle for foreign policy; nor was his principle "isolationism," that abusive term coined by the advocates of a grandiose American intervention in Europe and Asia. (Robert Taft stood upon the general principles of international law, repeatedly reaffirming them; and, with his father, he had recommended American membership in the League of Nations.) When he entered the Senate, he was (as he said) a "noninterventionist": that is, he took it that American national interests, and indeed the interest of international order, would be served best by avoiding European quarrels and alliances. Yet he never subscribed to the notion that the United States could ignore altogether the other governments of the world, or that the condition called "isolation," *per se*, could be converted into a diplomatic premise and desideratum.

Taft came to recognize limits to the postulate of the national interest; he learned that in an age of fanatic ideology, sometimes assistance to allies or to a common civilization must take precedence over the immediate national interest, narrowly interpreted. He desired, too, a comity of nations, governed by definite principles of justice, to which great states voluntarily should subordinate national appetites. But in the absence of an international order, and with allowance for the claims of a nation's allies and for military necessity, the national interest remained the only sure ground for the conduct of foreign relations.

Taft was no provincial: he knew well the power and the intricacy of the world beyond American frontiers. His service with the Relief Administration in Europe, from 1918 to 1919, had taught him early something of the complexity of the concerns of nations—and had taught him the enormous devastation inflicted by modern war. Even when he entered national politics, he was no doctrinaire "isolationist": he understood that intervention, or nonintervention, must depend upon the interest of the United States at a particular time, in varying circumstances. The conditions of America, of Europe, and of Asia altered mightily during his years in the Senate; so the gradual alteration of Taft's position in foreign affairs scarcely is an "enigma."

Taft's opposition to American entrance into the Second World War, all his subsequent positions in foreign policy, and his concept of the true national interest were strongly influenced by two prejudices (using that word in its neutral sense): his prejudice in favor of peace, and his prejudice against empire—that is, against American aspirations toward hegemony over much of the world. The misunderstanding that Taft was "inconsistent to the point of inconceivability" or that his conduct in foreign affairs was enigmatic, may be diminished by a brief description of these two prejudices—or two deep convictions—to which he was constant.

War, Taft perceived, was the enemy of constitution, liberty, economic security, and the cake of custom. His natural conservatism made him a man of peace. He never had served in the army himself, and he did not relish the prospect of compelling others to serve. Though he was no theoretical pacifist, he insisted that every other possibility must be exhausted before resort to military action. War would make the American President a virtual dictator, diminish the constitutional powers of Congress, contract civil liberties, injure the habitual self-reliance and self-government of the American people, distort the economy, sink the federal government in debt, break in upon private and public morality. The constitutions of government in America were not made for prolonged emergencies; and it might require generations for the nation to recover from a war of a few years' duration.

If these would be the consequences of war to America— even though no hostilities should occur within American territory—the damage inflicted elsewhere in the world would be graver still. Even though war might be inevitable in the last resort, men must not expect large benefits to result from

victory. From the Second World War, as from the First, no
increase of liberty and democracy would come: on the contrary, in most of the world a host of squalid oligarchs must be
the principal beneficiaries, whatever side might win. For the
United States, then, war was preferable to conquest or to
economic ruin; but if those calamities were not in prospect,
America should remain aloof. The blood of man should be
shed only to redeem the blood of man, Taft might have said
with Burke: "the rest is vanity; the rest is crime."

Taft's prejudice in favor of peace was equaled in strength
by his prejudice against empire. Quite as the Romans had
acquired an empire in a fit of absence of mind, he feared that
America might make herself an imperial power with the best
of intentions—and the worst of results. He foresaw the grim
possibility of American garrisons in distant corners of the
world, a vast permanent military establishment, an intolerant
"democratism" imposed in the name of the American way of
life, neglect of America's domestic concerns in the pursuit of
transoceanic power, squandering of American resources upon
amorphous international designs, the decay of liberty at home
in proportion as America presumed to govern the world: that
is, the "garrison state," a term he employed more than once.
The record of the United States as administrator of territories
overseas had not been heartening, and the American constitution made no provision for a widespread and enduring imperial
government. Aspiring to redeem the world from all the ills to
which flesh is heir, Americans might descend, instead, into a
leaden imperial domination and corruption.

With these convictions of Taft in mind—his attachment to
the principle of the national interest, his love for peace, his
detestation of empire—his course in foreign policy may be
surveyed more intelligently. Although it would be historically
interesting to survey his stand on a multitude of questions in
foreign relations from 1939 to 1950, only a summary is possible
here, without embarking upon a diplomatic and military history of that period. More, what Taft said and did during that
time is important, so far as his general principles of politics are

involved, only as background for his writings, speeches, and influence during the concluding two and a half years of his life.

For Taft did not become a power in foreign affairs until early in 1951, when he succeeded reluctantly to the dying Arthur Vandenberg as Republican spokesman on international matters; and when he was compelled to speak out systematically in this field because it appeared most probable that he would become the next Republican presidential candidate, in an election to be fought chiefly over diplomatic and military policy. (Taft did not take a place on the Foreign Relations Committee until his last year in the Senate.) For a decade, he had left Republican leadership in foreign policy to Senator Vandenberg—though often with serious misgiving and private disagreement over Vandenberg's "bipartisanship." During those years, Taft could not speak with authority even for his party; besides, he was in opposition to the Executive, and enjoyed no prospect of forming positive foreign policy—at best, he might hope to impose some check upon the Roosevelt and Truman administrations. So it was unnecessary for him to present, until 1951, a coherent alternative in foreign affairs; nor, indeed, could he have found time, amidst his complex work on economic and labor problems, to outline the complete foreign policy, running counter to the State Department's, which his hostile critics assume he should have presented.

What remains of enduring interest in Taft's thought on foreign policy, then, either was developed or was argued more systematically from the end of 1950 onward. Still, it may diminish confusion to set down, in the following section of this chapter, a summary account of Taft's positions on foreign relations from 1939 to the end of 1950.

Confronting War and Imperialism

During Taft's first year in the Senate, it became apparent that the Roosevelt administration was beginning to drift toward involvement in the Second World War. Checked in domestic innovation, the New Dealers grew increasingly interested in action—possibly short of war, but also possibly involving force, if the American public might be persuaded—against the Axis powers. (It was only through the stimulus to the nation's economy from supplying the Allies and engaging in military production, indeed, that the Roosevelt Recession was terminated.) Senator Taft promptly set his face against this movement.

Germany, he believed, then constituted no real menace to American liberty, or even to the American economy; while Fascist Italy, taken in isolation, was merely absurd. Although his sympathies were with Britain, France, and their allies, and although he disliked the military clique in Japan, in the beginning he advocated strict neutrality. Nazism was only an ideology in embryo, without appeal to Americans; but the ideological power of the armed doctrine of Communism, as represented by Soviet Russia, was a matter of grave concern for the United States. American intervention in the war might assist, inadvertently, the spreading of Communism; and he did not believe that Germany could altogether subdue Britain. So long as it seemed possible that the war might be terminated by a compromise settlement or in the defeat of Germany, without American intervention, he opposed assistance to Britain and her allies.

As the terrible strength of the Nazi regime became manifest, however, Taft commenced to shift away from strict neutrality toward some degree of American intervention, although still sternly resisting direct participation in the war. He voted for repeal of the arms embargo; although he opposed the Lend-Lease program (considering it a virtual declaration of war), he advocated as an alternative an American loan of two billion dollars to Britain, Canada, and Greece. He not only supported the National Defense bill of 1939, but recommended a program of military expenditure, including an appropriation for six thousand aircraft, exceeding the Administration's military budget. He endorsed, too, in 1940, the proposal for a two-ocean navy and the increase of the army to 375,000 men.

Taft's general attitude toward American involvement from 1939 through 1941, he explained in a lengthy letter to George F. Stanley, an Ohio manufacturer, written on September 8, 1944:

"My position during the years 1939, 1940, and 1941 was based on three principles: first, that we should stay out of the war unless attacked; second, that we should build up our defense to meet any possible threat of attack; third, that we should aid Britain as much as possible, consistent with the policy of staying out of the war. This policy was exactly that professed by President Roosevelt and Wendell Willkie in the campaign of 1940, *after* the Germans had broken through in France. I did not change my mind after the election and I thoroughly disapproved of the President's persistent efforts after the election to involve us in war while professing a policy of peace. I recognize that there was a sound argument for us to enter the war, but that argument was just as sound in 1940, before the election, as it was afterwards. In fact, when Russia became involved the possible danger to this country was considerably reduced.

"I may add that I have always been in favor of joining a league of nations on the theory that by joint action taken early to prevent aggression, a world war may be prevented in which we might become involved. I supported such a league in 1920 and fully agreed with the position taken by my father at that time. But it is two different things to prevent a world war, and to join a world war after it has been brought about without our fault or participation. The only justification for entering the war was the claim that if successful Hitler would attack the United States. My own belief was that such an attack could not have been made successfully provided we built up our defense forces, and particularly our Navy. President Roosevelt himself said on January 6, 1941, 'even if there were no British Navy it is not probable that any enemy would be stupid enough to attack us by landing troops in the United States from across thousands of miles of ocean, until it had acquired strategic bases from which to operate.' How could those bases have been acquired if we built a navy sufficiently large?"[4]

Taft favored a loan to assist Finland but opposed the American occupation of Iceland;* for the first was aid short of war, the latter a military relief of the British garrison. He was willing to grant substantial aid, short of war, to China. His last important vote on the eve of American entry into the conflict was against repeal of the cash-and-carry provisions of the Neutrality Act: for such repeal, he believed, would be perilously close to military alliance with Britain.

The Japanese attack on Pearl Harbor left Taft and his party with the duty of supporting the American cause in a war they had tried to avert. Taft himself was no very competent analyst of strategy and tactics, but while voting for every bill calculated to achieve victory, he asserted the duty of Congress to scrutinize the conduct of operations and to restrain the Executive from unnecessarily diminishing domestic freedom in the name of military expedience. As Taft put it later, "members of Congress, and particularly members of the Senate, have a constitutional obligation to re-examine constantly and discuss the foreign policy of the United States."[5]

A useful analysis—though somewhat chilly toward Taft, still more nearly impartial than most such studies of his attitudes before and during the Second World War—was published by Vernon Van Dyke and Edward Lane Davis in 1952, tracing Taft's movement, after America had entered the war, toward security through international organization. Taft came to argue, these writers remark, "that the United States should henceforth seek 'a rule of law and order in international relations.' He urged that the United States 'agree, under

* Taft feared that the occupation of Iceland, in 1941, soon would be followed by an American seizure of Ireland, to secure it for the British. (Letter of Taft to Herbert Hoover, July 16, 1941; copy in Robert A. Taft Papers, the Library of Congress.)

specified circumstances, to use our armed forces to prevent aggression, even though the determination of the fact of such aggression is left to an international body in which we are a minority member.' He envisaged no veto. He did, however, wish the American obligation to use its forces outside the western hemisphere to be a secondary one which would come into play only after regional agencies proved unable to keep the peace. And he fixed a number of prerequisites for American participation in a vetoless United Nations, including a 'revision of the world code of international law,' economic arrangements which would 'eliminate the causes of war,' and the thorough application of the principle of self-determination in the peace settlement."[6]

As Van Dyke and Davis point out, Taft's attachment to collective security of this sort was diminished, presently, because of the danger to domestic freedom from commitment to international decisions. "Taft can favor collective security as long as war is remote, but when a crisis occurs he is inclined to recoil because of the dangers to liberty which war would involve."[7]

The war aims of the United States were ill defined by the Roosevelt administration, Taft believed. And when victory came, he saw with dismay that Soviet Russia was being conceded more than she could have won by force of arms. He spoke out against many of the terms of the Teheran, Yalta, and Potsdam agreements. His post-war positions were summarized by W. Reed West in one of the comparatively few friendly articles in journals of opinion during that period:

"After the war, Taft worked earnestly for an association of nations based on laws agreed upon in advance. He objected strenuously to the failure to base the United Nations on an ascertainable law, and to the veto of the big powers. He believed the veto provisions rendered the organization helpless to prevent war except perhaps among little nations. He opposed NATO because he believed it inconsistent with the United Nations, because its terms were broader than a pledge to protect the signatory nations against Russia, and because he believed it committed us to the type of land warfare in Europe that he considers unwise. He opposed the Nuremberg trials. He has opposed any efforts to abandon Formosa to the Communists and sees no reason why we should have refused to use troops from Nationalist China to aid Americans fighting in Korea. He was dubious about the Marshall Plan while it included aid to Russia, but supported it after the Russian menace became clear and aid to the Soviets was eliminated."[8]

When the Korean war commenced, in June 1950, Taft supported action through the United Nations against the North Korean invaders, though he sternly criticized President Truman for dispatching troops without the consent of Congress. The failure of the United Nations promptly to condemn China for intervention in Korea, or to take decisive action against China, however, much decreased his confidence in that body. He accused the Truman administration of having failed to prepare for the defense of Korea, and of having virtually invited the North Korean attack by Dean Acheson's declaration, early in the year, that Korea lay outside the sphere of America's vital interests in Asia. While a Korean armistice was in prospect, Taft was writing the little book which became his most closely reasoned statement on foreign policy, and which will be examined in the next section of this chapter.

Taft's most spirited defense of his conduct during and after the Second World War may be found in his "Foreign Policy Statement" of April 24, 1952. Sherman Adams, a Republican politician then governor of New Hampshire—and then, as later, not celebrated for narrow scruples—had attacked Taft ferociously in the heat of the competition of Eisenhower and Taft for the presidential nomination: he had accused Taft, in substance, of being an erratic ignoramus in foreign policy, and a disguised liberal in domestic policy. Taft's reply was perhaps the angriest of his political life—but convincing. After repeating his arguments in support of his opposition to President Roosevelt's foreign policy, Taft turned to his own conduct after victory over the Axis powers:

"As for my record since the Second World War, I am free

to admit that I think we have poured out millions of dollars more than ever we should have done. Today, I would undoubtedly give away less of our taxpayers' money to foreign countries than Mr. Adams or his friends. It would be hard for them to prove that we have gained anything from the Bretton Woods Agreement. It cost us about $4 billion, and the Stabilization Fund has not stabilized. The World Bank is a minor operation in the world's economy. The loan to Great Britain has gone down the drain.

"Governor Adams simply falsifies when he says that I opposed the Marshall Plan. I felt that an emergency existed in the growing Communist threat which justified aid to anti-Communist countries. I have usually voted for economy, because I think about twice as much has been spent by the E.C.A. as was really necessary. Many of their projects have been most effective in assisting these countries to recover from the war, but there was also a tremendous amount of waste of both money and personnel. I voted for reasonable cuts in the various appropriations, but otherwise supported the Plan. . . . Today, I am inclined to oppose further economic aid, except for technical assistance, and programs to deal with specific emergencies like famine in India, or an influx of immigration into Israel. I do not think that perpetual financial assistance is good either for the country which extends it or that which receives it.

"Governor Adams stated that I voted against 'participation in the United Nations.' The fact is I voted for the United Nations Charter. I did point out, however, that the veto power renders the UN innocuous against a large aggressor—as has since been proved. I did oppose a bill setting up our representation in the Security Council, because it gave the President power to take this country into war through his control of the vote of the American representative; whereas I thought that any vote involving us in war should be first approved by Congress under our Constitution.

"As for the North Atlantic Pact, few realize that this treaty obligates us for the next twenty years to assist any nation

which is attacked by any other nation, even another member
of the Pact. It is simply an old-fashioned military alliance. I did
favor a clear declaration to Russia that, if she attacked any of
these nations, they would find themselves at war with the
United States. That would have left us a free hand to act in
our best interests at the time, and would have had the same
effect as the Atlantic Pact in deterring Russia from starting a
war. . . .

"I may add that, since we have entered into this treaty by
constitutional process, I believe we should carry out our
obligation. I am in favor of completing the arming of European nations, and voted to send six divisions to Europe to
encourage and assist them in building up the necessary armed
forces.

"Adams has made various other false charges in various
statements. He said that I 'proposed that the defense program
be reduced after the start of the savage war in Korea.' Of
course that is nonsense. I voted for the increase requested in
the Army immediately after Korea and frequently thereafter.
I did object to the further increase of expense to a point where
it would endanger our free economy and the productive
system here at home necessary as the backbone of our ultimate
defense. There is a wide difference among military men as to
what is necessary to assure our security. My suggestion then
was that, if we eliminated waste, we ought to be able to get the
same results with three million men as the Joint Chiefs of Staff
proposed together with three and a half million men. I said
that I thought that a total budget of $70 billion was the
maximum we could stand, even in an emergency. As a matter
of fact, in the present year we are only going to spend about
$65 billion, although Mr. Truman is still threatening to spend
$85 billion next year. In any event, the force I proposed was a
great deal larger than we had at that time.

"Adams lied about my position when he said that I 'used the
floor of the Senate to attack a 70-group Air Force.' I have
always supported a large Air Force, larger than we actually
have had."[9]

Sherman Adams's distortion of Taft's positions was a gross example of the treatment Taft's recommendations in foreign policy frequently received from journalists and academic critics, as well as political rivals. It was, and is, easy enough to detect minor inconsistencies and omissions in Taft's stand against the foreign policies of Roosevelt and Truman; but so it would be with any principal politician of that time, speaking hurriedly in the midst of tremendous events—and especially a politician in opposition to the Administration, sometimes denied access to confidential information and always under the necessity of rallying a disheartened minority in Congress.

Certainly Robert Taft's opinions regarding degrees of American intervention abroad, military and economic measures to deal with Germany or Russia or China, and international organization to secure the peace, underwent a variety of changes between 1939 and 1951. Had he not been able to change his mind in response to the challenge of events, Taft would have been an obdurate and ineffectual senator. Yet his general principles of concern for the national interest, opposition to war except as the final defense of American liberty, and suspicion of America's expansion of influence to every country, were not altered by his adoption of new approaches in foreign policy: he changed his front from time to time, but not his ground.

Taft's considered judgments on the conduct of American foreign relations are better discerned in his speeches beginning in 1951, and in his book *A Foreign Policy for Americans*, than by a hurried survey of his record during the preceding dozen years. He never had held a diplomatic post nor had enjoyed the confidence of the Department of State; so it was with some misgiving that he found himself, early in 1951, charged with the duty of formulating a positive foreign policy to set against that of the Truman administration. "People have accused me of moving into foreign policy," he told the annual convention of the Chamber of Commerce of the United States, in April, 1951. "The fact is that foreign policy has moved in on me."[10] William S. White, a little earlier, had asked Taft about his plans for foreign policy. "A shadow fell over his face and he replied: 'I wish I could just stay out of that; but of course I can't.' "[11]

Whatever Taft's deficiencies in this field during 1951, 1952, and 1953, he offered a clearer and bolder alternative to the policies in effect since 1939 than had Dewey or Willkie; and his frankness contrasted strongly with Eisenhower's vague and melioristic comments on foreign affairs. (Taft was much disquieted by Eisenhower's political naïveté, throughout 1952 and early in 1953.*)

The Struggle against Communist Arms and Ideology

Unattractive to him though the realm of foreign policy may have been, Taft set about his new responsibility with his accustomed vigor. Throughout 1951, he demanded a more energetic prosecution of the war in Korea, supporting General MacArthur; he recommended diversionary attack on the Chinese mainland by Nationalist Chinese troops from Formosa, with American backing. American security depended more upon the fate of the Far East than upon western Europe in 1951, he argued. The United States was fast losing ground before Soviet Russia; only a courageous assertion of American leadership, and a demonstration of American armed strength, he said, could prevent the Communist ideology from swelling into an immediate menace to American freedom. Perhaps the

* Taft appears to have noted somberly Eisenhower's testimony, in 1945, before the House Committee on Military Affairs. General Eisenhower then had told the Committee, "Russia has not the slightest thing to gain by a struggle with the United States. There is no one thing, I believe, that guides the policy of Russia more today than to keep friendship with the United States. . . . I am sure in my own mind there is in Russia a desire and continuing concern for a lot that we have in common, and they want to be friends with the United States." (Testimony of General Dwight D. Eisenhower, November 15, 1945, U.S. Congress, House Committee on Military Affairs, *Hearings on H.R. 515, Universal Military Training,* 79th Congress, 1st Session, 1945, pp. 78, 80.)

best specimen of his speeches during this period is his address to the American Assembly, on May 22, 1951.

Taft told his audience that the United States was over-committed in Europe; the pressing danger rose in Asia. "I do not believe that the fundamental issues regarding our relations with Europe present differences of principle but rather differences of degree and emphasis," he concluded. "Perhaps, however, there is some degree of difference with my basic principles which I here restate: My view is that American foreign policy should be directed primarily to the protection of the liberty of the people of the United States, and that war should only be undertaken when necessary to protect that liberty, that we are not justified in going to war simply to increase the standard of living of the people throughout the world, or to protect their liberty unless such protection is necessary for our own defense.

"Because of the power of Soviet Russia and the Communist philosophy, we must today do everything possible to prevent the extension of that power as a threat to our security, and are therefore interested in protecting liberty throughout the world. We have, however, certain definite limitations on our capacity and have to be selective in choosing the means to carry out our policy if we are not to wreck the American economy and the American morale. Broadly speaking, we can control the sea and air throughout the world and protect island nations and probably Africa, but we cannot control the land masses of Europe and Asia. This country can defend itself even though it loses control of those land masses. In order to assure our control of sea and air, we should maintain a close and friendly alliance with the British. While as part of our general policy we should give every assistance to France, Italy, Germany, Belgium, Holland, Denmark, and Norway, we cannot safely commit our entire efforts or most of our army to battle on the continent of Europe, any more than we can undertake an invasion of China.

"I believe the power of the United States is such that we can be safe if we use that power effectively, but there is one policy and only one policy which can destroy this nation—the commitment to projects beyond our capacity to fulfill. Germany is in ruins because Hitler thought he could conquer the world when he could not do so. Italy was wrecked because Mussolini thought he could create an Italian empire. We cannot permit any emotional affection for other nations to divert us from the policy of American security."[12]

The previous apparent willingness of Truman, Acheson, Marshall, and other members of the Democratic administration to abandon the Asiatic mainland, if need be, in order to concentrate American energies upon the defense of Europe, was a fundamental difference between the foreign policy of Taft and that of the Democrats in office; this argument runs through the book he was to publish late in 1951.[13] In October, Taft formally announced his candidacy for the Republican presidential nomination, and the Asiatic war became a chief topic in his campaign. Ironically, perhaps, Dwight Eisenhower, the candidate of the "Eastern crowd" that Taft distrusted, in 1952 would insure his election to the presidency by his declaration, "I will go to Korea." Taft was to lose the nomination but to shape Republican policy.

Taft's only book, *A Foreign Policy for Americans*, was published at the height of the Korean "police action." Although much of the press expressed dissatisfaction with this volume, it sold well and exerted immediate influence. On December 29, 1951, Taft wrote to his sister that he paid little attention to press comment, favorable or unfavorable, upon himself. He expected to make some $25,000 from his book—though most of that sum would go to the Treasury. "I have been rather pleased with the results because, while there have been plenty of criticisms, they don't seem to me to really upset any of the theory that I advance."[14]

In his foreword, Taft made a strong *prima facie* case against the Truman foreign policy:

"In 1945, when Mr. Truman became President, the Soviet Union was exhausted. Much of its industry was destroyed. It had no atomic bomb, no long-range bombing planes, no serious navy. Its hold on eastern Europe was shaky. China was our ally and the Chinese Communists were hemmed into a small area.

"President Truman held such power as no man had ever held before. Our air force was incomparably superior to any other. Our navy was more powerful than the combined navies of the rest of the world. Our army was a superb fighting force at the peak of efficiency. Our industrial plant, by far the greatest in the world, was intact. We alone had the atomic bomb which guaranteed the speedy destruction of any nation that might dare to risk war with us. We could have seized and held the initiative for the creation of a free and powerful world. Our leaders did not know how or where to lead.

"Today Stalin has atomic bombs and long-range bombers capable of delivering them on the United States. He has 175 Soviet divisions, and 60 satellite divisions in Europe, and a Chinese Communist army of about 3,000,000 in Asia. He has about 50,000 tanks and more than 15,000 tactical aircraft. His Indo-Chinese accomplices are draining the strength of the French Army. His guerrillas are withstanding the British Army in Malaya. He has riveted an iron control on eastern Europe. China is his ally. To face Stalin's 225 divisions the Western democracies and ourselves are scheduled to have thirty divisions in Europe—perhaps—by the end of 1951. Moreover, Soviet psychological warfare has been so successful in western Europe that one fourth of the French and one third of the Italians vote Communist. . . .

"Unless our foreign policy is conducted more competently than it has been during the past ten years, our very survival is in doubt. There may be infinite arguments as to the wisdom of many steps in our foreign policy since 1943. But there can be little argument as to its results."[15]

The purpose of American foreign policy, Taft contended in his first chapter, is to maintain the liberty and peace of the people of the United States; it is no practical aim of foreign policy to raise the living standard of all the world, or to secure freedom in every land. "Certainly if World War II was undertaken to spread freedom through the world, it was a failure."[16]

American economic and military assistance to foreign governments must be based on the need to avert "a real threat to the security of the United States." America should maintain "a free hand to fight a war which may be forced upon us, in such a manner and in such places as are best suited at the time to meet those conditions which are changing so rapidly in the modern world." Therefore American ground troops should not be kept in Europe in such large numbers as to disable America's general defense in the event of a disastrous land war in Europe.[17]

Taft proceeded to assert the right and the necessity, in the American democratic republic, for Congress to participate with the Executive in the conduct of foreign affairs: "If in the great field of foreign policy the President has the arbitrary and unlimited powers he now claims, then there is an end to freedom in the United States not only in the foreign field but in the great realm of domestic activity which necessarily follows any foreign commitments. The area of freedom at home becomes very circumscribed indeed."[18] Nor must the President be permitted, without the consent of Congress, to subordinate American interests to directives of the United Nations Organization: "If the President can carry out every recommendation of the Security Council or the General Assembly supported by the vote of the American representative whom he can direct, then he has almost unlimited power to do anything in the world in the use of either troops or money. . . . On the same theory, he could send troops to Tibet to resist Communist aggression or to Indo-China or anywhere else in the world, without the slightest voice of Congress in the matter. If that could be the effect of an international treaty, we had better watch closely the approval of any such treaty in the future."[19]

Yet Taft did not mean to separate the United States from the United Nations. The United Nations Charter suffered from the omission of any clear principle of justice: "I believe that in the long run the only way to establish peace is to write a law, agreed to by each of the nations, to govern the relations of such nations with each other and to obtain the covenant of all such nations that they will abide by that law and by decisions made thereunder."[20]

Without the rule of law, peace and security sometimes are not worth having. The United States had not given to the United Nations that example of respect for principles of justice which was so greatly needed: "The brazen disregard of law in the Korean enterprise and in the setting up of an international army in Europe is further evidence that our State Department has long since repudiated any serious respect for law and justice. It is now dominated far more by the philosophy of the economic planner who feels that the Government must decree the life of its citizens and of the world on a strictly opportunistic and expedient policy. My own feeling is that this policy in the field of foreign affairs, unless restrained, can only lead to arbitrary and totalitarian government at home, as foreign affairs come more and more to dominate our domestic activities, and to war in the world."[21]

What with the veto provision in the Security Council, and other weaknesses in the Charter of the United Nations—which should be amended, if possible—the United States could not rely upon the United Nations to prevent aggression: the Atlantic Pact had been a recognition of this hard truth. Therefore the United States "must develop our own military policy and our own policy of alliances, without substantial regard to the non-existent power of the United Nations to prevent aggression."[22] Conceivably the nations of the Atlantic Pact might concert "a new form of international organization based on law and justice without veto" to settle all disputes among themselves.[23]

Taft went on to describe how the Russian menace had been made possible through the feebleness of American policy—by the Teheran, Yalta, and Potsdam agreements. Roosevelt, Hopkins, Harriman, Wallace, Davies, and other New Dealers—to put matters mildly—had been "led into a complete misconception of the real purposes of the Russian Government and its communist character."[24] So, too, it had been with American policy in Asia. "The Far Eastern Division of the State Department was inspired, to say the least, by strong prejudice in favor of Chinese Communists, and that seems to have been shared also by Secretary Acheson himself. General Marshall was sent to China to insist that Chiang Kai-shek take Communists into his cabinet, and he did his best to force that result."[25] Taft felt that, as a result of these American diplomatic blunders, "Russia is far more a threat to the security of the United States than Hitler in Germany ever was."[26]

How might the Russian menace be confronted successfully? Containment could not suffice; there must be manifested an "affirmative power" of liberty. Taft offered seven recommendations for basic strategy:

"1. The creation of powerful American armed forces.

"2. Economic aid to countries where such aid will enable anti-Communist countries to resist the growth of Communism from within.

"3. Arms aid to countries where such aid will enable anti-Communist governments to resist aggression from without or armed Communist forces within.

"4. Warnings to Soviet Russia or its satellites that armed aggression beyond certain lines or against certain countries will be regarded by the United States as a cause for our going to war.

"5. The sending of American troops to a country threatened by attack from Russia or its satellites (European army) or where the attack has already occurred (Korea).

"6. An ideological war against Communism in the minds of men.

"7. An underground war of infiltration in Iron Curtain countries."[27]

All this was a far cry from the "isolationism" of which Taft so often had been accused. He recommended air power, primarily, as America's best defense; possessing sea power also, and in alliance with Britain, the United States might deter any government from attack—without maintaining more than strategic land forces, chiefly to protect lines of communication by air and ocean. Amidst all his Senate business, Robert Taft had found time to read much about the Napoleonic wars; and the military policy which he recommended was markedly similar to Pitt's successful strategy in that age. The British had "established garrisons at strategic points where sea power could protect them. It was the sea power of Britain which gave Britain a powerful influence on the continent of Europe itself.

"It seems to me that by reasonable alliance with Britain, Australia, and Canada the control of sea and land can establish a power which never can be challenged by Russia and which can to a great extent protect Europe, as it has been protected for five years through fear of what sea and air power can accomplish against Russia. There is no need for a specific line of defense in every section of the world, but we can exercise a power for peace over a vast area. If the Russians realize that our power in the final outcome cannot be challenged except on the continent of Eurasia, and perhaps not there in the final issue, and that it can do real damage to their own nation with the atomic bomb and otherwise, their purpose of military aggression in Eurasia itself may well wither. If they are convinced that they cannot achieve world conquest by military means they are likely to turn to their old love of propaganda and infiltration. Gradually, peaceful relations in Europe may grow again, for the desire of human beings for peace and comfort and normal human relations is a powerful force which will constantly assert itself."[28]

In Europe, the Russian threat could not be met with sureness of victory if we should rely upon a massive American garrison—not with the Russians already only eighty miles from the Rhine. Although Taft had opposed the establishment of the North Atlantic Treaty Organization, considering it a violation of the spirit of the United Nations Charter, now he was willing to arm the governments of western Europe if they should desire armament; but not to station many American divisions in Europe. In population and in economic resources, western Europe was potentially, if not immediately, capable of self-defense. "We are, of course, interested in the defense of western Europe, but it is beyond our capacity unless the Europeans provide not only the bulk of the troops but also the bulk of the interest and initiative, and finally take over the responsibility."[29]

Senator Taft concluded this chapter by remarking that he was less alarmed than some by Russian military power. "Our limited resources," nevertheless, must be utilized carefully. "I do not believe that western Europe can be defended unless the western Europeans are determined to defend themselves and will take the initiative in the rearming which is essential for that purpose. To encourage that action we are furnishing them with economic assistance and military equipment in practically any amount they can use. We will support them by sea and land, and I would agree to send some troops to prove to them that we do intend to fight at their side if Russia attacks. But even the program which I outline will require tremendous sacrifices from the American people, from every taxpayer, from every family, from every boy."[30]

As for the Russian menace in Asia, the failure of the United Nations to act against the Chinese invasion of November 1950 proved that America and her Asiatic allies or potential allies must rely upon their own strength. It might have been possible, once, to evacuate American troops from Korea; it was so no longer, for Japan and the Philippines must be endangered at once by the immense consequent gain of prestige by the Communists. We must not abandon the Nationalist Chinese in Formosa; on the contrary, we must shore them up as a principal bulwark of resistance against Communism and of American security. The Chinese Communists must not be admitted to the United Nations; even to withdraw unconditionally from Korea would be better, if the choice must be made, than to open the way for total Communist domination of the Far East.

"Broadly speaking, my quarrel is with those who wish to go all-out in Europe, even beyond our capacity, and who at the same time refuse to apply our general program and strategy to the Far East. In Greece we moved in with overwhelming support for the Greek Government, even though it at first had strong reactionary tendencies. . . . But in China we hampered the Nationalist Government. We tried to force it to take Communists into the Cabinet. The State Department spoke of Communists as agrarian reformers and cut off arms from the Nationalist Government at the most crucial time. Contrary to the whole theory of the containment of Communism, where it could be done without serious cost or danger, the Administration proposed to surrender Formosa to the Communists and has constantly flirted with that idea. . . .

"Certainly our program in Europe seems to me far more likely to produce war with Russia than anything we have done in the East. I am only asking for the same policy in the Far East as in Europe."[31]

Military power alone could not contain nor diminish the threat of communism, Taft wrote in his final chapter. Communist ideology was the more insidious enemy of freedom. He recommended a "positive campaign in behalf of liberty." The yearning after freedom had not vanished even behind the Iron Curtain. "And when I say liberty I do not simply mean what is referred to as 'free enterprise.' I mean liberty of the individual to think his own thoughts and live his own life as he desires to think and to live; the liberty of the family to decide how they wish to live, what they want to eat for breakfast and for dinner, and how they wish to spend their time; the liberty of a man to develop his ideas and get other people to teach those ideas, if he can convince them that they have some value to the world; liberty of every local community to decide how its children shall be educated, how its local services shall be run, and who its local leaders shall be; liberty of a man to choose his own occupation; and liberty of a man to run his own business as he thinks it ought to be run, so long as he does not interfere with the right of other people to do the same thing."[32]

The American struggle was not only against the Russian state, but against Communism—although many American politicians did not perceive this. "Thus, Secretary Acheson only a year ago stated: 'To say that the main motive of American foreign policy was to halt the spread of communism was putting the cart before the horse. The United States was interested in stopping communism chiefly because it had become a subtle instrument of Soviet imperialism.' With this point of view I emphatically disagree. I believe that we should battle the principles of communism and socialism and convince the world that true happiness lies in the establishment of a system of liberty, that communism and socialism are the very antithesis of liberalism, and that only a nation conceived in liberty can hope to bring real happiness to its people or to the world."[33]

So if Taft admired William Pitt's strategy, he shared with Edmund Burke the conviction that the real enemy was "armed doctrine," not old-fangled national rivalry. He outlined four steps for striking a counter-blow against Marxist ideology: first, "a world-wide propaganda on behalf of liberty," in which the Voice of America was a beginning; second, infiltration of Communist-dominated countries by secret agents, particularly exiles; third, buttressing those nations which believe in liberty and are prepared to do battle against Communism; fourth, elimination from the American government of "all those who are directly or indirectly connected with the Communist organization."[34]

The struggle against communism must be won in men's minds. War, rather than advancing liberty, generally establishes tyranny. "Communism can be defeated by an affirmative philosophy of individual liberty, and by an even more sincere belief in liberty than the Communists have in communism. In the United States we see the product of liberty to be the greatest and most powerful nation the world has ever seen, with the happiest people. If we rise to the power of our strength, there has never been a stronger case to present to the world, or a better opportunity to dissolve its darkness into light."[35]

Taft in Retrospect

One may doubt whether *A Foreign Policy for Americans* advanced Taft's candidacy for the Republican presidential nomination. "O that mine adversary had written a book!" Both the Democrats and the Republican liberals promptly endeavored to expose fallacies and inconsistencies in the little treatise—even though none of the critics had himself ventured to write a book about the debatable land of foreign policy.

To find ambiguities, minor inconsistencies, and omissions was quite possible. Did or did not Taft believe that the Russians were able to drop atomic bombs upon the United States? There existed some discrepancy here, on two different pages. His attitudes toward the Atlantic Pact and the North Atlantic Treaty Organization were not wholly clear. He said the defense of Korea was justifiable, and yet attacked President Truman's "brazen disregard of law" in dispatching troops without consulting Congress. As the editors of *Collier's* wrote, "We should not dwell too much on the discrepancies, for they are greatly outweighed by the senator's unequivocal statements."[36] But *Collier's* did not much relish some of the forthright declarations, either. Evasion and ambiguity often are considerable advantages to a presidential candidate, especially when a nation is at war.

Yet whatever Taft's opponents might say of his book, the fact remained that he had possessed the courage and the honesty to publish a manual of his convictions.* No other aspirant to the presidency in that year could or would express himself so clearly on foreign affairs. The Truman foreign

* Also, like his speeches, the book was altogether Taft's own work; unlike most eminent contemporaries, Taft did not lean upon the ghost-writer.

policy had been conspicuous chiefly by two features: the "Point Four" program of economic and military aid to a congeries of countries, with no standard to measure its own achievement and often of dubious efficacy; and last-hour military dashes to rescue what had been nearly lost through previous vacillation and imprudence. If Taft's recommendations in foreign affairs were unsatisfactory to some close students of international affairs, what might be said of Truman's hasty improvisations, or of Eisenhower's and Stevenson's generalities?

Taft's chief immediate achievement in foreign policy was to restore congressional debate over the conduct of American foreign relations. Bipartisanship in this field virtually had expired by 1948, but as late as 1951 President Truman still was asking the opposition not to criticize publicly his foreign policies. The notion of "bipartisanship" assumes that the President and the Department of State are omniscient, and that there can be no honest dispute as to what course the nation should take in its diplomacy and its military policy. By implication, during the Truman years, Taft dissented from the course which Arthur Vandenberg had followed in this matter during the Roosevelt administration. Taft put it thus in 1951:

"If we permit appeals to unity to bring an end to criticism, we endanger not only the constitutional liberties of the country, but even its future existence. . . . I think there ought to be a continuous discussion of [foreign] policy during this session of the Senate. . . . It is part of our American system that basic elements of foreign policy shall be openly debated. It is said that such debate and the differences that may occur give aid and comfort to our possible enemies. I think that the value of such aid and comfort is grossly exaggerated. The only thing that can give real aid and comfort to the enemy is the adoption of a policy which plays into their hands as has our policy in the Far East. Such aid and comfort can only be prevented by frank criticism before such a policy is adopted."[37]

Some liberal advocates of "bipartisanship" during the 1930's and 1940's now have come round, emphatically, to Taft's position that the Senate, in particular, should discuss with some candor the measures being undertaken by the President and the Secretary of State—and especially in the Far East.

Taft's practical recommendations remain controversial. Whether Taft, had he been elected President, would have succeeded in giving flesh to his convictions in foreign relations—that question raises conjectures beyond the scope of this book. President Eisenhower and Secretary of State Dulles, once in office, in part became converts to Taft's doctrines; had Taft lived somewhat longer and remained master of the Senate, doubtless they would have been pulled even closer to him.

Much of what Taft predicted or dreaded came to pass, within a dozen years after his death. In part from force of circumstance, in part from policy, America's struggle against the Communist powers did shift, in large measure, from Europe to the Orient. Communist ideology and Communist subversion diminished in power in western Europe, until in 1966 Dwight Eisenhower, from retirement, recommended that American military forces in Europe be reduced to two divisions; and in that part of the world, the United States came to rely upon missiles, aircraft, and naval forces for the defense of America's allies against Soviet ambitions—as Taft had recommended. Yet in the Far East, the primary employment of air and sea power, and the collaboration with Nationalist China—which Taft had proposed for sound policy in that quarter—were not realized: instead, a half-million American men, the vast preponderance of them inexperienced conscripts, became enmeshed in a land war in Southeast Asia.

The grandiose programs of foreign aid, which Taft had thought extravagant and sometimes baneful, grew increasingly suspect in Congress, and eventually were diminished somewhat, as the American balance of international payments became affected, as many states used such grants imprudently, and as the connection of the foreign-aid program with the American national interest seemed increasingly tenuous. By 1966, the criticisms of foreign aid once expressed by Senator

Taft could be heard on the lips of such liberal Democrats as Senator William Fulbright and Senator Wayne Morse.

The United Nations, as the years passed, was clearly exposed as impotent—Taft had said it must be—to settle disputes in which major powers were involved; and when that organization intervened in petty states, as in the Congo, its actions were ineffectual and damaging to the United Nations' reputation. America increasingly relied upon the augmentation of her own military strength and upon alliances—the policy Taft had suggested in his final speech.

With the increase of the prosperity of western Europe, the North Atlantic Treaty Organization diminished in influence, and Europe—France especially—began to assume that independence of action and armament which Taft had thought best for both Europe and America.

The wistful expectations of liberals that some satisfactory accommodation might be arranged with Communist China were disappointed, as Taft had declared they must be frustrated; and China swelled into a greater menace to the peace than Soviet Russia had been, and commenced to develop her own atomic weapons. Taft was vindicated by events in his dispute with Dean Acheson as to whether Soviet imperialism or Communist ideology was the real enemy; for the Communism which arose in China, or in such "emergent nations" as Indonesia and the Congo, was fiercer than that of Russia.

In retrospect, then, Robert Taft appears to have been more of a realist in foreign affairs than were many of his opponents, in either party; and much of the ridicule heaped upon him by the foreign-affairs optimists of his day, during his last three years, now rings hollow. Much has occurred, nevertheless, that Taft did not foresee.

He assumed, for instance, that American hegemony over the Caribbean never would be seriously challenged; yet Cuba was taken by the Communists only a few years after Taft's death, and very nearly became a major base for Russia. (Where Cuba was concerned, Taft presumably would have acted more promptly and decisively than did Eisenhower or Kennedy.)

Taft took it for granted, too, that the United States would remain in cordial alliance with Britain, reserving to the British their old spheres of influence, for the most part; he might have been startled at American intervention against Britain, France, and Israel (for which last state he had strong sympathies) in the Suez crisis.

The prolonged American assistance to such belligerent Socialist dictators as Sukarno, Nkrumah, and Nasser would have been almost incomprehensible to Taft. The confused and vacillating course of American policy in Laos and Vietnam would have roused him to sober remonstrance. The domination of the General Assembly of the United Nations by the Afro-Asian bloc presumably would have caused him to think again about the power of veto in the Security Council.

Still, Taft was more canny in foreign policy than many of his generation believed him to be; and historians of international relations, some years from now, probably will recognize that Taft possessed greater foresight than did such diplomats, in either party, as Chester Bowles and Henry Cabot Lodge. The principle of the national interest, the prudent endeavor to maintain peace, and the shunning of imperial grandeur remain goals of American foreign policy long after windy talk about "One World" has ceased even to amuse.

Notes, CHAPTER VIII

1. William S. White, *The Taft Story* (New York, 1953), p. 142.

2. For some strong comments on dogmatism in foreign policy, see Herbert Butterfield, *Christianity, Diplomacy, and War* (Lon-

don, 1953), Chapter 8, "Ideological Diplomacy *versus* an International Order."

3. John P. Armstrong, "The Enigma of Senator Taft and American Foreign Policy," *The Review of Politics*, Vol. 17, No. 2 (April 1955), pp. 230–231.

4. Robert A. Taft to George F. Stanley, September 8, 1944; printed in Taft, *A Foreign Policy for Americans* (New York, 1951), pp. 122–127.

5. Robert A. Taft, Speech in the Senate on the President's State of the Union Message, 82nd Congress, 1st Session, Vol. 97, Part 1 (January 5, 1951), p. 55.

6. Vernon Van Dyke and Edward Lane Davis, "Senator Taft and American Security," *The Journal of Politics*, Vol. 14, No. 2 (May 1952), pp. 183–184.

7. *Ibid.*, p. 183.

8. W. Reed West, "Senator Taft's Foreign Policy," *The Atlantic*, Vol. 189, No. 6 (June, 1952), p. 51.

9. Robert A. Taft, "Statement of Foreign Policy," April 24, 1952; a press release or (more accurately) an article printed as a five-page advertisement in Massachusetts newspapers. It was reproduced in part, and reported, by *The New York Times*, April 27, 1952, p. 34.

10. Robert A. Taft, address to the Annual Convention of the Chamber of Commerce of the United States, April 30, 1951; copy in Robert A. Taft Papers, Library of Congress.

11. White, *The Taft Story, op. cit.*, p. 148.

12. Robert A. Taft, "United States Relations with Western Europe Viewed within the Present World-Wide International Environment," address to the American Assembly, May 21, 1951; printed in the *Congressional Record*, 82nd Congress, 1st Session, 1951, Vol. 97, Part 13 (May 22, 1951), p. A2934.

13. For a recent detailed account of the Communist conquest of China, and of American policy at that time, see Anthony Kubek, *How the Far East Was Lost: American Policy and the Creation of Communist China, 1941–1949* (Chicago, 1963).

14. Robert A. Taft to Helen Taft Manning, December 29, 1951. Helen Taft Manning Papers, Library of Congress.

15. Taft, *A Foreign Policy for Americans, op. cit.*, pp. 7–8.

16. *Ibid.*, p. 17.

17. *Ibid.*, pp. 18–20.

18. *Ibid.*, p. 23.

19. *Ibid.*, p. 33.

20. *Ibid.*, p. 39.

21. *Ibid.*, p. 41.

22. *Ibid.*, p. 44.
23. *Ibid.*, p. 46.
24. *Ibid.*, p. 52.
25. *Ibid.*, p. 56.
26. *Ibid.*, p. 60.
27. *Ibid.*, p. 66.
28. *Ibid.*, p. 79.
29. *Ibid.*, p. 100.
30. *Ibid.*, p. 102.
31. *Ibid.*, pp. 112–113.
32. *Ibid.*, p. 115.
33. *Ibid.*, p. 117.
34. *Ibid.*, pp. 117–120.
35. *Ibid.*, p. 121.
36. Editorial, "But, Senator, They Don't Fit," *Collier's*, Vol. 129, No. 3 (January 19, 1952), p. 70.
37. Taft, Speech in the Senate on the President's State of the Union Message, January 5, 1951, *op. cit.*

CHAPTER IX

Taft and Permanence

WITH MANY political labors unfinished—for he was given merely a few weeks' notice—Robert Taft died of cancer on July 31, 1953. His courage, cheerfulness, and sense of humor—this last frequently evident in private all Taft's life, though seldom perceived in public—endured to the end. "He was about the best loser I have ever seen," said one of the doctors who attended him. "He gave us all a lesson in how to die."[1]

Despite his skill in practical politics, Taft had lost a number of political struggles; three times he had sought earnestly his party's presidential nomination, and three times he had been rejected. Yet he was victorious in death. Some journalists abroad were startled at the praise of Taft, dead, from men who had opposed him bitterly enough in life. (Foreign observers often fail to understand how American partisanship rarely is ideological in character, and how, therefore, five very different Americans who had won the presidency, or who were to win it—Hoover, Truman, Eisenhower, Kennedy, and Johnson—could unite in appreciation of the dead leader of party.) As Senator Lyndon B. Johnson said then in his eulogy, difference with Robert Taft "was the kind of disagreement which gentlemen could discuss without rancor."[2]

Some of the posthumous praise of Taft, nevertheless, was

192

fulsome and may have been hypocritical. President Eisenhower was sincerely grieved, for he had suffered a genuine loss. But what of the expressions of sorrow from some of Eisenhower's backers in the Republican contest of 1952, among them a number of eminent journalists? The phrase "a tragic loss" sounded somewhat odd on the lips of gentlemen who, during the Republican convention in Chicago, had intoned sanctimoniously through loudspeakers the words "Thou shalt not steal"—with the implication that Taft, who had given to his party more than had anyone else, was engaged in a shabby conspiracy to purloin the nomination he could not acquire by right.

John F. Kennedy, then junior senator from Massachusetts, spoke well for most leading men in both parties, however, in what he said of Taft. "Sometimes a nation's illustrious dead remain among its most influential men. Their character and personality are sometimes so strong and all-pervading that their influence continues to endure after death. . . . For his valiant effort to be to America what Churchill is to Great Britain; for being so right in his mind that he kept the respect of those of us who thought him wrong in some of his ideas; for showing the Nation how a man who is big enough to deserve victory knows how to take defeat; for the inspiration his career must be to all those who share in his patriotic aspirations—I nominate for the man of the year the late Senior Senator from the State of Ohio—Robert A. Taft."[3]

Whatever Taft's disdain for pandering to the crowd, his personal following was very large and strongly devoted; his abrupt end dismayed them. And even more Americans, not passionately concerned in party struggles, were saddened by the disappearance of the politician whose integrity had represented the best in the American commonwealth. The incorruptible man, says John Jay Chapman, will find his nook in time: "Honesty is the greatest luxury in the world, and the American looks with awe on the man who can afford it, or insists upon having it."[4]

Taft's party, and the Senate, have not since found his peer.

As Joseph Alsop—who had not been an admirer, ordinarily, of Taft's politics—wrote in August 1953, "You have to go a very long way back in American history—perhaps as far as the time of Clay and Webster—to find the American political scene being dominated and influenced in the Taft manner by any political leader who did not have the resources of the White House at his disposal. What made Taft's achievement all the more remarkable was that his power stemmed directly from his fine qualities. Those who disagreed with him, just as much as those who agreed, had to acknowledge his strong character, inexhaustible industry, hatred of sham and pretense, and deep Americanism."[5]

For fifteen years, the American public had sensed that Robert Taft stood for permanence in the United States: for what must be made to survive in a time of troubles. Taft spoke for constitution, self-government, private rights, the rule of law, security, peace, community, economic stability, the fabric of civilization. He had contended against ideology, concentrated power, grandiose political designs, imperial aspiration, class hostility, economic folly, the rootless mass age.

What he had prevented being done mattered more than what he had himself accomplished. A leader of the opposition leaves few statutes bearing his name, although Taft's labor legislation would last and would be strengthened by his successors.

Unendowed with much eloquence to give him a place in the copybooks, lacking executive decisions to evoke his memory in manuals of American history, will Taft's reputation endure? Of all the members of Congress who have sat in Washington since 1789, perhaps a score continue to influence discernibly the American mind and the American character. Taft was not picturesque; nevertheless, he will not be forgotten quickly. His portrait hangs in the Capitol, one of five—those senators chosen by a Senate committee as outstanding among all who have sat in the Senate of the United States. And the Robert A. Taft Institute of Government acquaints the rising generation with the high practical politics of which Taft was master.

His achievement, unlike Taft himself, was subtle. For Taft succeeded, in more ways than one, in resisting what had been called "the wave of the Future." Better than anyone else, he had given fresh strength to the conservative strain in the American character, and had wakened many to the difficulties of the mass age. With Burke, he had known that change is the means of our preservation; yet that healthful change must be in harmony with the historical experience of the nation.

He had revived a political party, and had restored a conscientious opposition in an age when parliamentary government had fallen into decay throughout most of the world.

He had stood, regardless of ephemeral popularity, for liberty under law—the liberties of all classes of citizens, in all circumstances. He had done much to restore full freedom to the United States after the exigencies of war.

He had spoken with effect against arbitrary power, and had affirmed in the twentieth century those principles of justice which many would have discarded on the pretext of expediency.

He had contended for a humane economy, in which the benefits of American free industry might be extended to everyone, without the oppressive weight of a socialist system.

He had done much to restore, in the public interest, the balance between management and labor, and had restrained by law the appetites of economic groups.

He had vigorously criticized the conduct of American foreign policy, and had regained for Congress some measure of influence over diplomatic and military affairs.

Few important members of Congress have accomplished a tenth so much. A campanile on Capitol Hill reminds senators that Robert Taft was among the greatest of their number; it is not so grand as the monuments of Washington, Lincoln, and Jefferson, but it signifies that Taft was not unworthy, in cast of mind and devotion to the commonwealth, of comparison with statesmen such as these.[6]

Their promise was fulfilled; given more years, Taft might have left as strong an imprint upon the American republic.

Responsible party, ordered freedom, power confined by law, a humane economy, a foreign policy founded upon enlightened national interest: these were his sober concerns, and he did not spare himself in his task. Because these principles which he upheld are among what T. S. Eliot called "the permanent things," some will repair to Taft in times of vertiginous change.

Notes, CHAPTER IX

1. Jhan and June Robbins, *Eight Weeks to Live: the Last Chapter in the Life of Senator Robert A. Taft* (New York, 1953), p. 23.

2. See *Memorial Services . . . together with Remarks Presented in Eulogy of Robert Alphonso Taft, Late a Senator from Ohio.* Eighty-Third Congress, Second Session (Washington, 1954), p. 26.

3. *Ibid.*, p. 190.

4. John Jay Chapman, "Society," in *Selected Writings of John Jay Chapman*, edited by Jacques Barzun (New York, 1957), p. 244.

5. Joseph Alsop, in the New York *Herald Tribune*, August 3, 1953; reprinted in *Memorial Services, op. cit.*, p. 217.

6. Tributes to Taft at the dedication of the Robert A. Taft Memorial, in 1959, are summarized in Phyllis Robbins, *Robert A. Taft, Boy and Man* (Cambridge, Massachusetts, 1963), pp. 272–276.

A Taft Chronology

September 8, 1889 Robert Alphonso Taft, eldest son of
William Howard Taft, is born in
Cincinnati, Ohio.

1900 Taft accompanies his father to the
Philippines, on William Howard
Taft's appointment as head of the
commission to establish civil government there.

Summer 1903 Taft sails home to enroll in his uncle
Horace Taft's Taft School for Boys,
at Watertown, Connecticut.

September 1906 Taft enrolls at Yale University. During
his years there, he becomes president
of the debating association, obtains
various academic honors, and is
elected to Phi Beta Kappa.

September 1910 Taft enters Harvard Law School, and
subsequently becomes editor in chief
of the *Harvard Law Review;* he
graduates first in his class.

1913 Taft passes the Ohio bar examination,
is admitted to the bar, and joins the
firm of Maxwell and Ramsey, in Cincinnati.

October 17, 1914   Taft is married to Martha Wheaton Bowers, in Washington, D.C.

1917   The first of Taft's four sons is born. Taft purchases a property at Indian Hill, near Cincinnati, and begins the development of Sky Farm, his permanent home. He twice tries to enter the Army, but is rejected because of his nearsightedness. He is selected as assistant counsel to the Food Administration, under Herbert Hoover.

1918   Taft serves in France as counsel, under Hoover, for the American Relief Administration. He is decorated by King Albert of Belgium, Premier Paderewski of Poland, and the Finnish government.

1919   Taft opens a Cincinnati law office in partnership with his brother Charles.

November 1920   Taft is elected to the Ohio House of Representatives.

1923   Charles and Robert Taft form a law partnership with John B. Hollister. The firm of Taft, Stettinius, and Hollister begins to develop into one of the most successful in Cincinnati.

1925   Taft is chosen Republican floor leader and president pro tempore of the Ohio House of Representatives.

1926   Taft is elected speaker of the Ohio House of Representatives. He accomplishes a new program of taxation for the state, and writes the Ohio Municipal Bond Act.

1930   Surviving a Democratic electoral land-
             slide, Taft is elected to the Ohio Sen-
             ate for a two-year term. He continues
             to work for tax reform, including re-
             peal of the old personal-property tax,
             and enactment of a new classified tax
             on personal property.

1932   Taft is defeated for re-election in the
             general Democratic victory; he re-
             turns to practice of the law.

1936   Ohio Republican leaders choose Taft
             as the state's candidate for the Repub-
             lican presidential nomination.

1938   Taft announces his candidacy for the
             United States Senate, and defeats
             Judge Arthur Day for the Republi-
             can nomination.

October 7–29, 1938   Taft debates with the Democratic in-
             cumbent, Senator Robert J. Bulkley,
             and wins the senatorial election by
             172,000 votes.

January 1939   Taft, commencing his first term in the
             United States Senate, is appointed to
             the committees on appropriations,
             banking and currency, education and
             labor; later the committee on finance
             is substituted for that on appropri-
             ations.

February 9, 1939   Taft introduces his first bill (S. 1275)
             in the Senate, to increase the amounts
             per unit permissible for housing loans
             under the Housing Act of 1937.

February 20, 1939   Taft ably opposes the appropriation for construction of the Gilbertsville Dam.

February 21—   Taft debates over a radio network with
May 16, 1939   Representative T. V. Smith.

March 6, 1939   Taft votes to increase the number of military aircraft to six thousand.

April 1939   Taft advocates repeal of the Arms Embargo Act, on condition that arms be exported only on a cash-and-carry basis.

July 26, 1939   Taft opposes President Roosevelt's "spending-lending" bill, and is successful; for the first time a major appropriation bill of the New Deal is defeated.

February 13, 1940   Taft votes against a bill for loans to Finland, because of danger to American neutrality.

March 20, 1940   Taft opposes increases in parity payments for farm crops.

April 18, 1940   Taft supports an increased appropriation for the navy.

May 22, 1940   Taft votes against the sending of aircraft to foreign governments.

June 11, 1940   Taft votes for increased American armament and military preparation.

July 1940   Taft, for the first time a serious candidate for the Republican presidential nomination, is defeated by Wendell

	Willkie at the Republican National Convention.
August 28, 1940	Taft votes against compulsory military training.
September 11, 1940	Taft opposes the enlargement of the lending authority of the Export-Import Bank.
March 7–8, 1941	Taft supports an amendment to the National Defense Act which would restrict use of American military forces to the Western hemisphere and to U.S. territories and possessions.
March 8, 1941	Taft proposes that a loan of $2 billion to Great Britain, Canada, and Greece be substituted for the Lend-Lease bill.
July 25, 1941	Taft protests the sending of lend-lease aid to the Soviet Union, ridiculing the "idea that Russia is battling for democratic principles."
August 5, 1941	Taft proposes eighteen-month enlistments, rather than indefinite extension of conscripts' period of service; his amendment is defeated.
December 8 and 11, 1941	Taft votes to declare war against Japan, Italy, and Germany.
February 5, 1942	Taft votes for enlarged financial aid to China.
July 6, 1943	By a single vote, Taft's motion to reconsider the continuation of the Commodity Credit Corporation is passed.

February 1, 1944   Senators Taft and Wagner propose (Senate Resolution 247) that the United States assist in the establishment of Palestine as a national homeland for the Jewish people.

March 21, 1944   Taft votes to authorize American participation in the work of the United Nations Relief and Rehabilitation Administration.

Summer 1944   Taft is chosen chairman of the resolutions committee at the Republican National Convention.

November 1944   Taft is re-elected as Senator from Ohio, defeating William Pickerel by the margin of 18,000 votes.

March 1, 1945   Taft opposes the nomination of Henry Wallace as Secretary of Commerce.

May 30, 1945   Taft delivers his first major address in opposition to universal military training—at Gettysburg National Cemetery.

July 18–19, 1945   Taft votes to postpone consideration of the Bretton Woods agreement until November 15; he opposes American participation in the International Monetary Fund and in the International Bank for Reconstruction and Redevelopment.

July 28, 1945   Taft votes to ratify the United Nations Charter—with reservations.

November 14, 1945   Senators Taft, Wagner, and Ellender introduce S. 1592, a bill to establish a permanent national housing agency and to make federal grants in aid of housing construction.

November 29, 1945   Taft is defeated in his attempt to authorize American representatives to the United Nations Organization to refuse to vote unless satisfied that justice will be served.

December 3, 1945   Taft votes to limit the power of the President to make treaties with the United Nations unless two-thirds of the senators consent.

May 3, 1946   With Senators Ball and Smith, Taft introduces S. 2143, a bill to establish an independent national health agency, and to authorize federal grants-in-aid to the states for public-health programs.

May 25, 1946   Taft opposes President Truman's bill to draft railroad workers then on strike, and causes the ultimate defeat of the proposal.

August 2, 1946   Taft supports the Connally Amendment, to restrict the American jurisdiction of the International Court of Justice to determination by the United States.

October 6, 1946   At Kenyon College, Taft criticizes the Nuremberg Trials.

January 1947   At the opening of the Republican-controlled Eightieth Congress, Taft becomes chairman of the Republican policy committee.

January 31, 1947   With seven co-sponsors, Taft introduces S. 472, a bill to provide federal grants-in-aid to the states for public schooling.

March 12, 1947   Taft votes in favor of a Constitutional amendment limiting tenure of the Presidency to two terms.

April 9, 1947   Taft opposes the appointment of David E. Lilienthal as chairman of the Atomic Energy Commission.

April 22, 1947   Taft supports the "Truman Doctrine" and votes to authorize the President to aid Greece and Turkey in their resistance to Communism.

June 23, 1947   The Taft–Hartley Act is passed over President Truman's veto.

July 18, 1947   Taft votes to override the President's veto of a bill reducing personal income taxes.

March 13, 1948   Taft supports the Marshall Plan—with misgivings.

June 1948   Thomas Dewey defeats Taft for the Republican presidential nomination.

September 23, 1948   Taft introduces a bill to establish a Fair Employment Practices Commission to reduce racial discrimination in employment.

April 29, 1949   Taft votes for the National Housing Act of 1949, chiefly an enlargement of his own housing bill.

July 21, 1949	With reluctance, Taft votes against the North Atlantic Treaty.
May 5, 1950	Taft opposes President Truman's "Point Four" program for economic assistance to "underdeveloped" countries.
September 23, 1950	Taft votes to override Truman's veto of the Internal Security Act of 1950.
November 1950	Taft is re-elected to the Senate by a margin of 430,000 votes, defeating Joseph T. Ferguson.
Fall 1951	Taft publishes *A Foreign Policy for Americans*.
April 2, 1952	Taft supports the "Tidelands" bill, giving seaboard states title to underseas mineral deposits.
April 15, 1952	In an address at Pittsburgh, Taft denounces President Truman's seizure of the steel industry.
July 1952	Taft is defeated by General Eisenhower in the contest for the Republican presidential nomination.
September 12, 1952	At Morningside Heights, Taft and Eisenhower confer; Eisenhower promises to support the Republican platform, and Taft to campaign for Eisenhower.
January 1953	Taft gives up his post on the Senate finance committee and moves to the foreign-relations committee; he also gives up the chairmanship of the Re-

publican policy committee and becomes floor leader.

May 1953   Entering Walter Reed Hospital, Taft
learns that he suffers from cancer.

May 26, 1953   Taft's last major speech, criticizing the
United Nations Organization and
Truman's policy in Korea, is read to
the National Conference of Christians
and Jews, in Cincinnati.

June 10, 1953   Taft resigns as floor leader and is succeeded by Senator Knowland.

June 12, 1953   Taft draws up his will.

July 31, 1953   Robert A. Taft dies in New York City.

Index